Being Jewish

Being Jewish

by Shimon Hurwitz

second, revised edition

FELDHEIM PUBLISHERS
Jerusalem

ISBN 0-87306-196-9
Published 1978
First edition, 1978
Second, revised edition, 1979
Second printing of second edition, with the appendices
    revised and updated, 1981

Designed by Charles Wengrov

Philipp Feldheim Inc.
96 East Broadway
New York, NY 10002

Feldheim Publishers Ltd
POB 6525 / Jerusalem, Israel

Printed in Israel

Dedicated to the everlasting memory
of our sainted leader and teacher
Rabbi Dr. Eli Munk זצ״ל
(London — Jerusalem)

who taught us by his example
the cheerful, stalwart and peaceful service
of the Holy One, blessed be He

Haskama by Rav Moshe Feinstein shlita

Having been an attorney-at-law [in the United States] in the past, afterwards Mr. Shimon Hurwitz drew near to Judaism and took to studying Torah at Yeshivat Dvar Yerushalayim, founded and headed by the noted Rav Baruch Horovitz. Now [as a result of this experience] his heart has inspired him to write a book in English, the *lingua franca* of this land, to explain and elucidate, in part, the concepts of haShem's Torah, as well as Jewish customs and laws, to those who have drawn near to the Torah of haShem and to those who desire to come close to haShem and His Torah. And I say that this is a very good thing, for as we know, today the generation is ripe for this, many having already found their way to Torah and religious observance in recent times; and his book will be of help and assistance [in this regard]. I therefore bless the author, that the Holy One, blessed is He, may grant him success with this work, and that his portion may be among those who further the righteousness of the Jewish people. And may he merit to do further great deeds in this field.

30 Shevat 5739 (1979)

RABBI MOSES FEINSTEIN

455 F. D. R. DRIVE

New York 2, N. Y.

—

OREgon 7-1222

משה פיינשטיין

ר"מ תפארת ירושלים

בנוא יארק

בע"ה

הנה כמר שמעון הורביץ שליט"א אשר כבר היה עורך דין ואחרי זה
נתקרב ליהדות ולמד כמה שנים בישיבת דבר ירושלים אשר יסד
הרה"ג המפורסם ר' ברוך הורוויץ שליט"א וכעת רחש לבו דבר טוב
והוא לחבר ספר בשפת אנגלית המדוברת במדינה זו להסביר ולבאר
קצת את מושגי תורת הד' ומנהגי ודיני ישראל לאלו שהתקרבו לתורת
הד' וגם לאלו שרוצים להתקרב לד' ותורתו ואני אומר שהוא דבר טוב
מאד דכידוע היום אכשר דרא והרבה התקרבו לתורה ויראת שמים
בזמן האחרון וספרו יהיה לעזר ולסיוע על כן אני מברך להמחבר נ"י
שיצליחיהו השי"ת בספר זה ויהיה חלקו ממזכי הרבים, ויזכה לעשות
עוד פעולות גדולות בענינים אלו.

וע"ז באתי עה"ח יום א' בהא/ו/ד/ו/ן תשל"ז

משה פיינשטיין

RABBI M. S. SHAPIRO
Dean

RABBI S. WOLBE
Principal

הרב מ. ש. שפירא
ראש הישיבה

הרב ש. וולבה
מנהל רוחני

ישיבת באר־יעקב

RABBINICAL COLLEGE YESHIVAT BE'ER-YAAKOV

BE'ER-YAAKOV, ISRAEL
HAYESHIVA ST.

Adar 5739

ב"ה, באר־יעקב,
רחוב הישיבה

Being Jewish is the first book of its kind, and it is to be hoped that more books of a similar nature will follow.

The author, having himself lived through the American cultural experience before entering the Torah world, is able to define and analyse the two contrasting life-styles, and by setting one against the other he demonstrates clearly the superiority of the Torah outlook. Thus, through a critical examination of modern society, the light of the Torah and its outlook is revealed—החושך מבחין את האור.

The importance of this book as an eye-opener to those not acquainted with the Torah life-style is obvious. However, this book is equally important to the *Ben Torah*, to clarify and highlight the supremacy of an unchanging but viable Torah life-style over a hollow, aimless modern culture, and to prevent him from being impressed with the outside world.

S. Wolbe

contents

Foreword

Behold, days will come — says the Lord God — when I will send a famine into the land: not a famine for bread, nor for water, but to listen and understand the words of the Lord. And they will wander from sea to sea and from the north to the east, they will grope around to search for the word of the Lord and they will not find it. But on that day will the beautiful maidens and the young men faint of thirst (Amos 8: 7-13).

Those days have come. We live in an age when young people all over the world are searching for the ground of being, the spiritual reality which forms the basis of the universe. A part of this movement is also to search for one's roots, universally, nationally and individually. The Jew of today is involved with an even deeper search for his true identity, which is bound up with the spiritual Guide of the nation of Israel. Unfortunately, many who grope searchingly do not find the truth of God and the genuine meaning of Jewish identity, because there are not sufficient channels of communication open from those who live in the light of Divine revelation, which has formed the secret of Jewish existence, to those who have grown up in spiritual darkness.

This book may become a means of showing the light to the young searchers amongst the people of Israel. It is written by a young man (a former lawyer) who was brought up in the average American culture and who came to Israel searching for spiritual roots and Jewish identity. He arrived at *Yeshivat Dvar Yerushalayim*, the Jerusalem Academy of Jewish Studies, four years ago, with wide interests and a deep understanding of life, but without much knowledge or commitment to the Jewish religion. Coming close to the world of Torah, he has been inspired and enlightened by the great teachings and practices of the Torah-world's life and has begun spreading this inspiration to others.

I am sure that there will be very many who through this book will find their spiritual thirst quenched. *Being Jewish* will make a great contribution towards promoting the *teshuva* movement, the movement of return to Torah values in our age, and thereby help to bring enlightenment to the whole House of Israel.

Rav Baruch Horovitz, M.A.
Rosh HaYeshivah / Dean
Yeshivat Dvar Yerushalayim /
The Jerusalem Academy
of Jewish Studies

Being Jewish

PREFACE

This book would never have come to be were it not for
several dynamic and concerned rebbeim whom the author
met at Yeshivat Dvar Yerushalayim / Jerusalem Academy
of Jewish Studies: Rav Baruch Horovitz, Rav Aryeh
Carmell, Rav Eli Munk צ״ל (London), Rav Mendel
Farber and Rav Menachem Goldblum. Their constant
dedication and warm efforts to help all Jews learn the true
meaning of being Jewish have inspired the author to the
understandings and ideas which he has endeavored to
express in this book. May it be Hashem's will that they,
and the rebbeim like them, so continue to kindle and fuel
the special flame in every Jew that the light created will
very soon bring the entire Jewish People and the whole
world to their true and final destiny.

I wish to express special appreciation to my wife for
her constant assistance; to Mr. Yaakov Feldheim for accepting this book under the respected aegis of his publishing house; to the Feldheim staff (particularly Mrs. Naomi
Goldblum) for the preparation of this book for publication;
and to Mr. Gershon Ginsburg, New York, for his help on
the list of Torah schools for beginners, which appears in
Appendix A.

... לא תלמד לעשות כתועבות הגויים ההם ‏(דברים יח ט)‏
אבל אתה לומד להבין ולהורות, כלומר להבין מעשיהם
כמה הם מקולקלים, ולהורות לבניך: לא תעשה כך וכך,
שזה חוק הגויים. ‏(רש״י; ועיין גם ספרי שם, ובבלי סנהדרין ס״ח)‏

... you shall not learn to act
according to the detestable deeds of those nations
(Devarim/Deuteronomy 18:9)
But you may learn [their vile practices
in order] to understand *and to* teach
— that is to say,
to understand their activities,
how corrupted they are,
and so to instruct your children:
"Don't do this-and-that,
because that is the established practice
of the nations."

(Rashi, based on Midrash Sifre and Talmud, Sanhedrin 68a)

10

Introduction

This book has one purpose: to reach out to the millions of Jews who do not know the true meaning of being Jewish.

The author is a Jew, a product of mid-twentieth century American culture. He, too, did not know what it meant to be truly Jewish. Through a series of events, he met people in Jerusalem who taught him what it means to be Jewish. Although very much still a beginner, he is so taken by the stark contrast between the western culture which he knew and the true Jewish culture he is now learning about that he is compelled to proclaim to all his brother and sister Jews that they should consider (or reconsider) their current Jewish identification. Whether their commitment to Judaism is non-existent, or marginal, or medium, or even strong, with Hashem's help this book may open new doors of awareness to every Jew who is mature, open-minded and desirous of growing.

The format used will be informal and not seek to inject the source material which the reader truly deserves to receive. The hope and prayer are merely to open a window in the mind of the western-culture Jew, to force the reader to examine his Jewish identity and to incite him to seek out the sources directly from the type of teacher whom the author has met and learned from.

There is no real beginning or end to this book, because it could potentially deal with the whole of existence, and, since such breadth is impossible, only a selection of topics will be dealt with, enough, it is hoped, to demonstrate the point: authentic Jewish culture and western culture are 180° apart.

One warning is necessary before we begin: by describing the two cultures on the same plane of reference, we solve one problem but create another. Because no falsehood can stand without some truth in it, western culture can appear worthwhile. So, by placing it on the same plane as Judaism, we accept that many Jews can be persuaded to view western culture (or whatever hybrids they create) as a viable alternative to authentic Judaism. But, in reality, the difference is not linear but three-dimensional. Judaism is as far above its seeming alternatives as life is to death. So the Jewish reader must *never* forget that whatever comparisons are made between Jewish culture and western culture, the truth would never allow the latter the opportunity to be mentioned in the same breath with the former. But to help the reader understand this fact, this book exercises "poetic license" by describing comparisons between the two cultures.

And with Hashem's help, we begin.

I

THE CORE OF THE CULTURE

The core of western culture can be expressed in one idea — the individual. He is the king. Whatever he likes, whatever is good for him, whatever he finds pleasurable is the center of the western value system. Moreover, he is free to decide on his own whatever he wants with few limitations. The most important question in life is: what does he want? Once he has decided, the decision attains instant validity because the individual and his wants are the ultimate goals.

Thus, the culture is geared to discover and satisfy the individual's desires. Polls are regularly conducted, from selecting a national leader to rating television programs, from the most effective aspirin to the catsup with the best tomato taste. Then huge resources are marshalled to cater to the winning desire. He wants to go bowling; so build him an 86-lane bowling alley. He wants to go driving; so build him a ton of metal and a million-mile road. On and on, round and round, until every possible desire is satisfied.

This last stop, of course, is never reached, because new desires are created, whether wrapped up in the guise of necessities, such as how can one live without an extension telephone in his bedroom, or patently tailored to appeal to the acquisitive instinct, such as "Wouldn't you really rather have a Buick?" The whole culture is so geared to the need to satisfy its appetites that people actually crave advertising that will tell them what they need (e.g., an electric ice chopper, a sit-down power mower) or what they can do with their time (e.g., a tour to the Greek islands, what movie is playing tonight).

The more sophisticated prefer more cultural interests, but these are no different in principle from the desire of the "hard hat" to enjoy his can of beer while watching football on TV. One craves political power, the other prefers contemplating a Rembrandt, while the third loves devising new mathematical equations. And so it goes: everyone is in life to see how much he can get out of it, how much he can enjoy it, how many of his tastes, desires, whims, fancies, dreams he can satisfy.

Mention must be made of that brand of idealism which challenges the mainstream. Such an idealist is driven by a desire to improve society, serve mankind, help the downtrodden, make the world a somewhat better place through his having been here. The thrust is outer-directed, and the "I" is seemingly muted.

This reaction to western culture is perfectly justified, but as a life pattern it has several weaknesses. The idealism often wanes as youth grows into maturity, matrimony, and mortgages. Outer direction alone does not solve the weaknesses of the individual's personality and character. And, finally, this altruism is still only an effort to express a personal need — the need to improve things, the need to make a contribution. The person still believes that man is the central purpose of the world's existence and that everything should be directed to taking care of him and his needs. Thus, again, the core value of western culture dominates the scene.

*   *   *

This book is not intended to be negative; on the contrary, its only purpose is to be positive. But in order to show the positive, the negative realities must be presented. That man is the center of all things is an absurdity beyond all question. For consider, what is man?

Biology dissects and atomizes him. Chemistry cans and packages him as a composite of mostly carbon, hydrogen, and oxygen compounds. Geology says that he is a very recent creature, almost a speck in the span of time. Archeology and history find him building up only to be torn down. Psychology deems him little better than a conditioned animal scurrying through a maze. Politics and government call him a "silent majority," paying his taxes and making vain choices between Tweedledum and Tweedledee. Astronomy sees him as drifting in a vacuum light years in diameter. Economics is convinced that he is a consumer who wants to work three days a week, be paid for five and still spend more money than he earns. Medicine considers him a machine that often malfunctions and ultimately succumbs to planned obsolescence. The arts express the malaise of this existence but leave him in the dust bin with no solution and only more confusion.

Looked at objectively, man is almost a waste of time. He lives seventy years. He sleeps and eats approximately 40% of that time, which leaves him forty-two years. For his first twenty or twenty-five years he is maturing and almost completely unaware of his role in life, either passing time away or preparing for life by studying a trade or profession. This total leaves him with 27 to 30 years of life. If we cut off the last five years for retirement time or the ailments of the declining years, we are left with a balance of around twenty-five years which a person has to use productively for life. Two and a half decades — that's all.

And let's say that everything goes his way and he adds on a few more years. He makes his fortune, becomes a respected and esteemed member of the community with a fine family, plaques of public recognition on the wall, the best country club membership and a four handicap on the golf course. One day, no matter what his bank rating, he lies ever so lifelessly under cold, damp dirt. What was it really worth that he made the valiant struggle to have everything he wanted?

Morbidity is not a Jewish trait. Realism, however, is, and this short but stunning blow to the life style of western culture should unmask the vanity of it all.

THE TORAH CENTER

A Jew's optimistic tendency is to make the best of the situation in which he finds himself. So, if his surrounding culture is vanity, he still tries to improve the world in his own way: work hard, raise a decent family, lend a helping hand. Thus, he copes with his plight by saying that he has done all he could under the circumstances. After all, life is no more than what it appears to be — a dead end. During his stay on this earth, he might as well have a good time and, while he is at it, do a good turn for his friend when the opportunity arises.

An individual who has not been exposed to any alternative to the "dead end" life style to which he has become accustomed is not likely to devise one on his own. The author certainly did not and would have remained stuck in his ignorance if a chain of events had not placed him in a yeshiva, a place of learning where Jews study Torah. Torah is the written and oral heritage of our Jewish forefathers, which has existed since before the world began and was given in its present form to the Jews at Har (Mount) Sinai, 3300 years ago. An alternative does exist to the emptiness and self-indulgence of western culture, and it is totally different from the way the assimilated Jew lives.

The core of Torah Jewish living is *not* the individual. The center for the Jew is Hashem (God), the Creater and Father of all.

Realistically, this Center makes sense. A result has no meaning without the cause. What is primary cannot be supplanted by what is secondary. What is ultimate, eternal and all-powerful must have precedence over what is miniscule, finite and impotent. It is logical and completely comprehensible to accept that there is a Creator, a Being far above man's conception who caused all to be and continues at this moment to cause all to be. It can be said that those who believe that the world merely happened by accident or chance — or even by a process of chance development — believe in a creation that is beyond the range of mathematical and biological probability.* If common sense is doubted, at least let us not ignore clear facts.

It is true that the self-centered nature of western culture effectively assists the delusion that the individual is the center and first cause of all things.

* Cf. Rav Aryeh Carmell and Professor Cyril Domb, eds., *Challenge: Torah Views on Science and its Problems*, Feldheim Publishers, Jerusalem, 1976, Section II.

But after we have already demonstrated that man's dominion is transient and temporary, anyone seriously examining the situation must realize and accept that a far more permanent center exists.

Most Jews, if pressed, would accept that Hashem exists, but they would deny or resist accepting that any personal relationship exists between Him and them. The Torah Jew, however, accepts not only that Hashem is the one and only Force in existence but also that the Jew achieves meaning and completion in life only to the extent that he becomes one with this Force. The Jew's individuality and personality are, therefore, not ends in themselves to be enhanced and made successful. Rather, they are means to an end, their true purpose being to perfect their relationship with the Creator.

Once one realizes that he really is not the most important being on this earth, he can come to accept that the really important Being must come first in his life. All that he is doing thereby is recognizing the reality of his position and the concomitant responsibility to respond to this reality. But this approach depends on whom he considers Number One. Western culture tells him that he is number one. The Torah Jew realizes that he is not number one. From this recognition he is ready to listen to and follow the desires and commands of the real Number One. The Cause and result, therefore, are intimately intertwined.

One further observation should hopefully uproot any thesis that man really is number one. Besides recalling his certain demise and disintegration, we have only to look at man's conception to conclude equally that that which is practically nothing cannot be considered number one. Specks of liquid protein smaller than a drop of water can produce a man six feet tall and weighing one hundred and eighty pounds. We have taken this miracle so much for granted that we have forgotten that we owe our very existence to a Force so far beyond our ken that it would be absurd if we acted as if we believed that man causes his own existence, that he is the center of all things. Hashem has brought us into existence and continues to give us life and direct our actions. He who is in the control tower is certainly not puny man, and he who mistakenly thinks so is not following the right directions. One might say, even, that he is missing the reason for which he was given existence.

This fundamental difference in orientation from man to Hashem being the Center of existence is the single most important distinction between the life the author experienced in western culture and the life of the Jew who follows Torah.

II

THE PATH TO FOLLOW

"All very well and good," one might say. "You live life the way you want, and I, the way I want. After all, look at all the different religions, philosophies, sects, cults. You think Hashem is the center of your existence. Fine. I have my own way, which I think is just as good, if not better. And since there are so many different paths to follow, you can't tell me that you're any more right than I am."

Western culture is pluralistic in ideologies. In fact, pluralism is one of its main ideologies. America epitomizes the ultimate in this approach because it contains so many divergent groups. It is an article of faith engraved in the American Constitution that everyone can do, think and say almost anything he wants. Indeed, the effort to impose one way of thinking and acting on everyone contributed to the migration from Europe and the rebellion against its influence.

Since, as a practical matter, no one right way can coexist with any other, western culture has concluded that there is no one right way to go. Whatever way the individual wants to live is completely satisfactory. Vegetarianism is as good as being religious; being a devotee of athletics is as good as collecting stamps; one likes hamburgers, the other political conventions. As a result, a person could conclude that any direction he takes is the right one, and who is to say otherwise.

His culture certainly encourages such an attitude. Parents do not know any right way and are content when others guide their children's path — teachers, counselors, friends. Schools, for their part, persistently claim that it is not their responsibility to teach the students what is right and wrong. They want only to make their students "well-rounded" and well-developed in their potential. Where this potential is supposed to go is not their business. Even though the purpose of education is to lead, after sixteen years of schooling, large lecture courses and small seminars, a private library of books and reams of term papers, the graduate can walk off the campus firmly grasping his diploma and not having the faintest idea where he is going.

It is true that we find gestures at defining goals and direction in life. But they are generally all vague and artificial. The valedictorian's address calls for high ideals, but his top-ranking company position considerably tarnishes his sincerity. The party nominee's call for action and sacrifice has so long been muffled in the back rooms of pay-offs, bribes, nepotism, and corruption that it is a wonder that any but the most naive still listen. The soporific pulpit sermons, apart from keeping people employed, so little reflect the guidance needs of people that everyone is struggling to make religion "relevant," but at the same time not changing the basic religion — the religion of "the choice is yours; do what you want!"

Since there is no right path and no one to follow and since people in reality need both, coping mechanisms are activated to allow people to pretend to make do under the circumstances. Lost in a fog, most sane people stop. But those who say that that is just the way life is convince themselves that there is no alternative to a chartless path even if mishap is certain to occur. Indeed, it is considered a mark of maturity to cope with a life that has no signposts, no direction, and no clear purpose. Thus, societal pressure pushes one further into the fog and deludes one into thinking that everything is fine.

Even so, some feel compelled to seek a purpose or an approach to life. In a hundred different ways, an individual tries to define his life. Perhaps he envisions a new world with social justice and equality, defending the oppressed poor and reforming all corruption. Or he has smaller hopes of building a solid home, a firm financial base, and sending his children to college. Maybe he will make his own new sub-culture which lives on soybean protein and free thought. Or he will open new avenues of intellectual or artistic endeavor. He will even try to mold a "new" Judaism to answer so-called "modern" problems.

Others drift along without any real purpose, content with drinking the morning cup of coffee, reading the newspaper and going to work. After all, what is wrong with the way the "Joneses" live?! To define or understand life as anything beyond a salary promotion, a television program, an exciting card game, the stock market, an office party is both unnecessary and a waste of time because (1) that is all that he is familiar with, and (2) everybody else is doing these things. Besides, between making a living and having a little fun, what else is life for?

Since no one in western society really knows what life is for, any answer or even no answer at all is completely satisfactory. Either, however, entirely misses the mark.

THE TRUE PATH

Again, with no special insight of his own, the author probably would have been content with "any answer or no answer." Following the group, with assorted modifications and idiosyncracies, is too persuasive a force to be counteracted by individual intuition or initiative. Habit and a measure of contentment block alternative life-styles to that of western culture. A steady salary muffles the mind. And nobody likes to rock the boat, particularly when in the absence of any other boats it is keeping him from sinking.

Even so, a certain gap must have existed because the author decided to find out more about what makes him Jewish, perhaps subconsciously realizing that more answers were needed; that since he was in reality ignorant of life's true path, he had to keep searching until he found it.

Other Jews, far more sensitive to life's dilemmas

and more discontent with accepting what is, would not question the constant need to search and are diligently working on life solutions of their own. Still others are content with life and feel no need to seek a truer path. A third group is on the fence, basically content but sensing that a better, more fulfilling Jewish existence must be possible. And, finally, there are many people who unfortunately have forgotten, ignored or denied that through pursuing their Jewishness in its true direction they could find greater meaning in life.

To all these Jews the following analogy is addressed:

You have built a computer after tremendous mental and physical effort. You are interested in selling it, and after a time you find a customer. He pays you, you wrap it up for him, and he takes it home.

When he arrives home, he unpacks it and takes out the instruction pamphlet which you provided in order that he should be able to use his purchase. It goes without saying that such a complicated apparatus as a computer needs instructions for operating it. And the customer would not think of pushing the first button without thoroughly studying the way in which it is properly to be used.

Life is infinitely more complex than any computer. Does it make sense to think that there is no instruction book? Clearly, if even something manmade requires directions for the user, then life, which is made by Hashem, must also come with instructions for using it. It is illogical to assume that the Planner-Designer-Creator of a world so fantastically complicated and so intricately coordinated would leave His "customer" unguided and uninstructed about how to use what he has been given.

When a teacher gives a test, he instructs the class on how to complete the exam. When a chef offers a recipe, the exact ingredients and directions are required for the best results. When men establish a society, a set of rules and procedures are ordained in order to ensure the proper functioning of the system. Is the Creator any less considerate?

Whether these examples are perfectly comparable is irrelevant. Their purpose is to represent a concept: *there is* a rule book from the Creator Himself on how to guide one's life.

If this principle does not appeal as common sense, then the many examples which this book hopes to present, with Hashem's help, will justify acceptance of this all-important foundation.

For who can look at the order of the universe, its stars and galaxies, the rotation of the earth, the balance of nature, the complexity and variety of life, and not conclude that there is a Planner and a Plan! Who can study the human being and not be awed at a design of such profundity and intricacy that obviously an Eternal Intellect is directing his path! And what Jew can see his long, troubled, but triumphant history and fail to realize that his very existence this day is a manifestation of a Divine Plan and Order!

And as will be seen, the Plan is not confined to the "law of nature," but extends to every particle of human behavior. Not just for once a year or once a week, but for every day and every second in every day.

III

THE EXISTENCE OF TORAH

Ask any bookdealer which book is the all-time best seller and he will immediately answer "the Bible." It is in almost every home and hotel room in America. It is in every language, every size, shape and model from paperback to leather-bound, with pictures, without pictures, thumb-indexed, gilt-edged — and even with a place to put in the family history. It is quoted in context or out of context every day. Its concepts and philosophy underlie all of civilized human thought.

So what does western culture do with this book? It places it on its library shelf along with all the other millions of books, pulls it out when necessary for speech material, college courses, court oaths, and puts it back — largely unread — as just another competing viewpoint in the marketplace of ideas. Sometimes enlightening, often provocative and certainly reputable.

The unknowing Jew, unfortunately, adopts his culture's superficial attitude, grafting onto it even further misconceptions: The stories of the Bible are fictional, often no better than fairy tales. The ideas and rules are the work of human intellect. It is an old book, better suited to the ancients than to cultivated, modern man. Other religions have bibles; so the Jewish one is similar and not particularly unique. The English translation is stilted and unclear; therefore, it *and* the Hebrew original are unworthwhile to read and learn. Finally, it has no greater claim of relevance or benefit for improving the quality of life than any other written work, from Shakespeare on tragedy to Doctor Spock on child care.

Moreover, many base their information about the Jewish Torah on completely second-hand and unreliable sources. A popular movie like *The Ten Commandments*, a television special on "the Bible," a newspaper feature, an occasional lecture or pulpit speech — such scattered fragments can actually be what people think is Torah. This misinformation combines with common assumptions to create the prevalent attitude that "all that Bible stuff is for religious people, and I'm not that way."

Finally, there is the Jew who admits a curiosity and interest in his Torah but just does not have time to learn more about it. Besides all his work and family responsibilities, he has so much to read already: (1) trade and professional literature, (2) newspapers and magazines, (3) the current best seller, (4) the classics, (5) hobby books, (6) light reading for a change of pace. Besides these, he must cram in a physical exercise program, an ample entertainment schedule and that yearly magic vacation to get away from it all. Now, how can he possibly have time to open up his Jewish Torah!

THE JEWISH TORAH

Jewish tradition says that Torah existed before the world and will continue to exist after the world ends; that Hashem looked into the Torah and created the world; and that if Jews stopped studying Torah, the world would cease to exist.

These are very strong statements, and probably incomprehensible to the Jew who has primarily been educated in secular schools and accustomed to the western-culture view that the Bible is just another book on the shelf. Put succinctly: the Torah is the Foundation, Blueprint, and Guidebook of the Jew's existence. As described before, the Creator established a path to follow so that His creatures would know how to use the complex life which they have been granted. This Instruction Book is called Torah and includes the Five Books of Moses (plus the Prophets and Writings) and the Talmud (Gemara).

36

The reader might ask how we know that this is true. Very simple. Historical fact. On the 7th of Sivan in the Jewish year 2448 in the Sinai desert at Har (Mount) Sinai, two and a half million Jews heard Hashem Himself utter the first details of this Instruction Book. This event, where so many people directly experienced Hashem, has no parallel in the history of mankind.

This fact is of tremendous significance, and the more one learns Torah the more he realizes it. Of course, if the Jew has not as yet had an opportunity to study, he may fail to understand or even challenge this truth, much like a layman denying the scientific theory of relativity.

A lot depends on how much the individual is open to new horizons of understanding. If he is content with his western-culture values, he will feel no need to change his conception of Torah. But if he is receptive, he will find out that Torah is:

— not of human origin, but directly from Hashem;

— the actual history and recurring experience of the Jewish people;

— the lifeblood of the Jewish people's continued existence;

— a solid, unbroken tradition of 3300 years, carefully handed down one generation to the next;

— not just the part called the "Bible" (the Five Books of Moses, the Prophets, and the Writings) but also twenty volumes of the oral explanation of the Torah, called the "Gemara";

— not a dusty antique, dotted with archaic

thous and *arts*, but a *revolutionary* program to perfect the Jew and to achieve his ascension to a new realm of existence;
—not a book shared in common with other peoples, but a completely separate and distinct body of thought and action reserved *only* for the Jew.

In addition to the historical proof of Torah, there are countless empirical proofs. The effort of this book is to let the reader examine a *few* of these in order that he will himself perceive that Torah is truth. All that he has to do is to be honestly searching for truth and responsive to the stark contrast between Torah and western culture.

IV

DEATH

"If you really want to live, drink Brand A soda pop and smoke Brand B cigarettes while flying on Brand C airlines to Brand D resort."

Life is something to be tasted, swallowed, experienced, enjoyed — so goes the western culture's central axiom. Since our physical senses know nothing more than physical stimuli, then that is all there is. This approach means that death is a "no-no," i.e., a topic not relevant to life, best left undiscussed and even unconsidered. After all, there are no physical pleasures after death, and it has no connection with the goal in life — a good time. Everyone agrees that death is definitely not a good time. So let's keep ignoring it and enjoy ourselves.

So what does happen to "death" in western culture? It is made a joke: "you'd be late for your own funeral"; "I'm going to die when my number is up — I just hope the pilot's number isn't"; "last night was really dead at the obituary news desk."

It is made a profitable business. Thousands of dollars can be spent on funerals and impressive graves. And life-insurance companies make millions with their actuarial charts.

It is made a mystical cult, an interesting college course, the climax of novels and tear-producing movies.

It is made, most of all, the silent enemy.

Distaste for it, combined with the emphasis on being young, has successfully eliminated death from the consciousness, except, of course, when it unavoidably intervenes. Then people get upset about it for a while but very quickly thereafter stuff it away in the attic closet of their minds, escaping further disturbance or anxiety. "What can you do about it anyway" is the reasoning, "and it ruins the good time we're having. So forget it."

Actually, all this sublimation is a bluff, and everyone knows it. Everyone over 45 or 50, that is. Someone at that age will die and suddenly they begin to think more about the topic. Then, in a few years, they find themselves scanning the newspaper's obituary column, at first just to note the details of a known departure but, gradually, to find out who else they know on the list. Before they read only the front page, the sports and the comics. Now they turn first to the obituary column. "Oh, I remember him from high school." "Say, only last month I saw her at the shopping center."

More poignant than this habit is the preoccupation with wills and bequests. From a legitimate concern to provide for loved ones, the death-sublimated individual imagines how it will be when he is gone and everyone will divide his wealth. Throughout, he avoids the personal reality of death by planning for the more pleasurable life of others. He has not managed to grasp the meaning of life and death, but maybe, with his money, his children will.

LIFE WITHOUT DEATH

Ignoring death is comparable to being in a river boat rapidly heading to a precipitous waterfall with jagged rocks and, despite knowing that a fatal disaster is ahead, gaily enjoying the ride, eating, drinking, and being merry.

Such behavior is, perhaps, the classic "escapism" — avoiding reality — and no one would deny that it is an unhealthy way to live. Most simply conclude that there is no other choice and attempt to make the best of a bad situation by reducing pain and increasing pleasure wherever and however they can.

But the most exciting thing for a Jew to learn as he studies what it really means to be a Jew is that there is an alternative to death, that the Jew does not die, but lives forever.

This idea is obviously totally different from the concept held by most Jews, that life has a dead end. The difference includes even secular notions that through children or memories left behind one can still live on. While these are certainly true, they are not what we are talking about here.

Originally, Hashem created man to live forever, but because man, in the exercise of his free will, decided not to follow Hashem's rules, he cut short his own life. Meaning: when one in any way rejects the Source of his existence, he immediately destroys part of his own existence. Reduce the electric wattage and the machine works less. Or, just as an employee who fails to come to work on time finds his salary docked (i.e., his source of livelihood is reduced, cut away), so, too, man had the potential never to lose his existence by becoming totally identified with the Source of his existence. However, when he rejected this opportunity he brought death into the world — the most severe state of distance from his Source. His lifeless corpse can no longer communicate with Hashem. Granted that his spiritual part has returned to its Source, the test was to see if, while alive, he could give all of himself — physical and spiritual — over to Hashem before Hashem took the opportunity away from him.

The first man — Adam HaRishon — had his Torah to do ("Torah" — that which Hashem commands His creatures), but for reasons which he thought justifiable he chose not to follow what Hashem told him to do. If he had listened, he would not have died. Today, the collective body of the Jewish People is in the place of Adam Ha-Rishon. If we follow our Torah, then death will cease. If we use the rules which Hashem has given us to live by, we activate the potential of converting ourselves from egocentric to Hashem-centric, from limited by our human weaknesses to exalted to the highest state of human perfection.

This potential to achieve eternity is just that — a potential, an opportunity. There is no write-your-own-ticket or guaranteed seat engagement. No magic words, no magic belief, no simple cures. The Jew gets his place in eternity according to the merit of the deeds which he has done. These deeds are judged not in quantity, but in quality; not simply how he used the qualities which he was given, but how he improved these qualities; not how he made excuses for his weaknesses in character and personality, but how he overcame these weaknesses.

Pursuing such a goal is extremely hard work, both internally and externally. When steel is made, iron ore has to be smelted in a furnace at enormous temperatures. When it comes out, it has solid strength. So, too, the individual. Life is a purification process, a constant testing-ground for the strengthening of a person's good side and the extraction and elimination of his bad side. To the degree that he succeeds in this battle, he connects with the Source, who is Eternal Existence, and thereby himself gains eternal existence. He overcomes death — ending — by reducing the amount of time that he denied the Unending One (by doing bad) and maximizing his complete identification with Him (by doing good).

So we see that a person gets what he strives for. If he does not want to die, he works very diligently at coming closer to the Source, understanding that he has only a limited amount of time in which to improve himself to his highest possible maximum. But if, like an ostrich, he ignores death and occupies himself very little with joining his Source, he cannot overcome death — his ending — because he has not worked to prevent his ending.

Life, then, is a preparation, a practice chamber, for entrance into a life of far greater significance and lastingness: a life close to the Source of all existence. If we use our reasoning just a little, we will realize that the slight, fleeting pleasures of this world have no significance and that our lives can be best used developing our potential to live an infinitely higher existence, one that can even defeat death.

V

"JUDAISM"

Everyone has his view of what "Judaism" is: It is the first religion to declare monotheism, and from it other religions developed. It is just another one of many religions of the world and, probably, just as good a "crutch" as the others whenever a weak mood strikes the individual. Its major distinction is in not recognizing the various gods of the other religions, but in essence it has the same purpose of making everybody treat his neighbor better. It has its own inherited customs and quaint traditions which people follow just out of habit — apparently a trait shared by many peoples. It may serve a function on certain occasions, such as a funeral or a Yom Kippur service, but most of the time it has no relevance to life. There is value in keeping it alive just as in preserving all artifacts, but that it has anything new and exciting to say is almost out of the question. Its best hope now is the modern country of Israel, which gives it a sense of pride and world-standing. Otherwise, with the general decline in synagogue attendance and increasing assimilation through intermarriage, it is probably, if not a dead letter, certainly of minor importance.

"Still, I would not deny that I am a Jew; indeed, I am proud of the fact. After all, it is only patriotic to subscribe to a religious denomination, just as one supports his local sports team or belongs to his community's civic action committee. And on an institutionalized level of membership — sisterhoods, brotherhoods, afternoon schools for the children — 'Judaism' has a definite social value, supplementing the professional association, literary club and golf foursome.

"And if 'Judaism' has become antiquated, it needs only to be updated. First off, nobody understands Hebrew; so almost everything should be in English. Separate seating of men and women is completely out of the question. There is not enough music in the services; so let's play a guitar during the Yom Kippur prayers. Everyone now admits that 'Judaism' has ignored the needs of women; so everything men do in the synagogue, women can do also. (What's wrong with women rabbis!) The prayers are too stilted; let's devise our own new ones, with blank verse and poetry, spiced with non-Jewish sources for a universal flavor. And the best way to attain respect among religions is to invite non-Jewish clergy to speak; then, no one will charge Jews with being bigoted or closed-minded. After all, only the accident of birth made each of us a Jew instead of a non-Jew.

"Moreover, it's a free world, and democracy requires individual choice. So every Jew has the right to decide how much 'Judaism' he wants in his life. If all that his 'Judaism' means is membership in the Jewish Community Center and a yearly contribution to the United Jewish Appeal, then, fine, that's all it has to be. If his 'Judaism' means going to synagogue once a week and on holidays, then that's all he has to do to complete his brand of 'Judaism.' And, although it may be stretching things a bit, let's even create a type of 'Judaism' without the Creator in it!"

Finally, a comfortable definition of "Judaism" is worked out, but even this changes to suit the mood. "Sure a ritual bath house (*mikveh*) is important, but the beautiful replica of the Western Wall in the front of the synagogue depleted the *mikveh*-building fund." "Because the seats for the High Holidays are so expensive this year, we'll skip going to services." "If dialogue with non-Jews is all right, what's wrong with intermarriage with them?" "I don't think I'll give so much money to Israel this year; the cancer society and heart association are certainly as important." "The Hebrew school studies are secondary to the children's secular education. After all, they can learn about 'Judaism' later if they are interested and have the time."

"Judaism" is the proverbial short-order breakfast: soft-boiled, sunny-side-up, scrambled, omelet, poached. Whichever way you want it served is fine. After all, it's all the same basic egg, isn't it?

TORAH JUDAISM

Contrary to the popular conception, Judaism is not a religion. It is a way of life. Not just for special occasions — bar mitzvas, weddings, funerals — but for every *second* of the Jew's life. Moreover, Judaism is not just an aspect of the Jew's life; it is the totality of it.

The necessity for such a total system of living is obvious once one recalls the opportunity which the Jew has to challenge death. Like a person suspended on a rope over a precipice, the Jew clings every moment to his Judaism because it enables him to preserve his life now and forever.

The Creator organized nature in an intricately ordered and balanced pattern — the cycle of water, photosynthesis, gravity, the laws of motion, the laws of radiation, the productivity of soil, food digestion, reproduction. The science of life is an endless revelation of unparalleled harmony and beauty.

Just as the Creator decreed a system and pattern for the natural world, He decreed a perfect order of living for man, the purpose of creation. Indeed, all objects in existence are only a backdrop for the action of this only free-willed being in the universe — man. But since Hashem's purpose was not to create another object or robot but rather a free-choosing human being, the plan decreed for man is not directly enforced on him because then, obviously, there would be no free choice. Nevertheless, a plan of living exists for him, and its name is Torah.

Like the other rules of nature, Torah
— operates all the time and covers every aspect of life;
— is unchangeable, unamendable and absolute;
— is totally perfect, complete and true;
— is violated at the risk of one's well-being;
— never harms but always turns out for the good;
— requires intense study, coupled with complete intellectual and emotional involvement;
— is so deep and unfathomable that, as much as it is understood, light years of understanding lie ahead.

Further, like nature's rules, Torah comprises a whole system of requirements, regulations and standards, each interconnected with and inseparable from the others. These rules are termed "mitzvot" (commandments) and are just as all-inclusive and binding on the Torah Jew as the laws of gravity, and just as essential for his health and full existence as the process of photosynthesis. An "eco-logical" nightmare would result if any one rule were rejected or replaced on the erroneous theory that Torah Judaism can be altered at will or that, as free-willed beings, we can determine the best way to run our immensely complex lives because of our "superior intellect" and "profound wisdom." The One who keeps the whole world hanging while it spins in space knows far better than we how life can best be lived.

In one crucial respect, Torah is not like the rules of nature. As mentioned, it existed before the world and will exist after the world ends. Meaning: Torah is above nature and completely connected to Ha-shem.

This fundamental distinction reveals the purpose of all the rules and practices. They are not just an approximate approach to being a good person and leading a good life. Torah Judaism is a *precise* system of thought and behavior constructed to bring man close to the Creator. Hashem made man im-perfect to give him the job of perfecting himself, with the Instruction Book (Torah) telling him how to do it. As man works to become more perfect, he moves closer to the Creator, who is All-Perfect. Since Torah is the definitive means to achieve close-ness to Hashem, it is itself a living aspect of the Creator, above time and space. It is a direct link with Hashem Himself, *provided* it is used as de-creed. It is to be followed exactly, much as one uses a map to reach his destination. Since in this case the journey is so difficult and so prone to error, the only sensible thing to do is to observe every sign-post, every marker, every instruction. Then — and only then — will the journey succeed.

VI

"I'M ALL RIGHT, SAM"

The western culture's approach that the individual is number one results in an essential corollary to the structure of the whole system. In order to be number one, the individual must convince himself that he already is almost as perfect as he possibly could be. In a society where everyone is number one, how can he survive if he does not present an image of confidence, self-esteem, self-satisfaction and know-it-all competence?

Not only is he forced to say, "I'm all right, Sam," but he soon convinces himself that, indeed, he is all right. The individual's public position thus plays back into his private character. Certainly he is not perfect, but he cannot afford to face this reality because it will not help him to think about his imperfections and it could even hurt him. Instead, his ego develops numerous defense mechanisms to protect its vulnerability from the reality of its weaknesses.

A thousand supports are at his disposal to prop up his situation. As a general rule, money is the surest protector of the self-image of perfection. Indeed, western culture is particularly prone to this defense mechanism, precisely because its high standard of living obviates examination below the surface. Only when a financial crisis occurs — loss of job, personal bankruptcy or professional blunder — does the individual feel any compulsion to examine his make-up and deficiencies. Otherwise, his bank account tells him that he is doing just fine!

If it is not the bank account, then a new car will do as a certain proof that he is a healthy success. Or maybe a new wardrobe, or a trip to the Caribbean, or an expensive necklace for his wife. Or maybe he can take out his wallet and show you all his credit cards or country club memberships or professional association affiliations or even pictures of his handsome family. Or let us walk into his office or den and survey all his diplomas, awards, citations, and trophies. These certainly say that he is a success, that he has achieved and is continuing to achieve all the basic expectations of his society. A true portrait of the American dream.

Of course, if we take away the veil of this dream, we find quite a different picture. He is alone: in order to show that he is invincible he has had to hide from everyone to prevent revealing his true self. He is insecure: he knows down deep that his public self does not reflect the reality within, a reality that is weak and constantly seeking reinforcement. He is angry: society has so strongly imposed its will on him to achieve the success image and his own real desires have become so completely frustrated that he is in a rage at the abuse to his personality. He is unhappy: as much as he has, he still wants more. He feels dishonest: his role-playing has become so dominant that he feels no truth inside and doubts if truth exists at all. He feels empty: all his success is outside and very little inside. He is upset: how could the success dream look so good and do so little to make him truly happy?

Finally, he becomes complacent and self-indulgent in order to escape the misery of his "success." He makes food, liquor or drugs a more frequent pastime. Other men's wives are no longer forbidden. Criticism of himself by others is completely intolerable. Self-examination has no time in his appointment book or play-time schedule. As the ultimate defense mechanism, he builds a walled fortress and resides in a castle full of rooms without content. And he is enthroned as the near-perfect picture of strength, achievement and truth.

HONEST SELF-EXAMINATION

A patient may be suffering from cancer, but he ignores the doctor's instructions because he imagines himself immune to the disease. So, too, an individual may pretend that he is near perfect and do nothing to correct the "cancer" within him. This "cancer" is his character weaknesses, poor qualities, and human imperfections. Instead of curing these internal diseases, he buys a new suit and walks around looking handsome and healthy. In the meantime, he is being eaten away from the inside and has sealed his end.

The Torah Jew realizes a fundamental fact of life: he was created imperfect, and his job is to perfect himself as much as he is able.

Realizing our imperfections is not very hard. We just have to look honestly in the mirror. We get angry and ill-tempered at times. We are stingy and hide from helping those who truly need assistance.

58

We are egocentric, ignoring or even stepping on fellow human beings. We love to dominate. We see other people as means to our own ends. We are selfish; we are jealous and envious of others. We speak ill of other people. We grab first for ourselves. We lust and chase after things that do us no good. We are lazy, bossy, bragging. We are heartless, childish, impatient. We fail to think of others' feelings. We lie and take what is not our own. We are haughty, cunning, overbearing, and convinced that our mistakes are really other people's fault. And we believe in our heart that we deserve so much more than what life is giving us. At the same time, we are vain and relish that contentment when our belly is full and all is well with us. We idolize power, the body, force, even when we know that they have caused only destruction and pain. Finally, even when we admit that we have some faults, we do little if anything to change them, choosing one or all of the following rationalizations: (1) that is just the way we are, for better or worse; (2) our weaknesses are really not that bad, particularly since others have similar ones; (3) on balance, we are still "nice guys"; (4) nobody is perfect nor is perfection a realistic goal.

For this very purpose Torah exists: so that man can achieve individual perfection and, thereby, the perfection of the world.

First, of course, we have to sense our inadequacies, be ashamed about them and feel a need to correct ourselves. The Jew in a Torah environment is encouraged to experience all these impulses.

He studies Gemara, which forces him to look truthfully and analytically at all thought and action. He does and learns the mitzvot of Hashem, which are designed to break his egocentricity and force a confrontation with his weaknesses. He has the constant support and guidance of parents, family and friends who expect of him the highest standard. He is continually exposed to examples of people whose lives and characters reflect the battle to improve themselves. He develops a close relationship with a teacher who motivates him on a personal level to correct himself. He is given the responsibility to teach and guide others, which forces him to improve the model which he is presenting. Instead of telling him that he is all right, his environment tells him to be honest, to examine his weaknesses and constantly to work on improving them.

All this process, as we mentioned, is in order that the Jew can reach a greater understanding of Hashem, the All-Perfect One. The Jew has this potential to perfect himself if he only works hard and consistently. Thus, the Torah world and western culture stand in direct contradiction. The latter convinces the individual that he is all right, while feeding him excuses why his deficient character and nature cannot and need not be improved. Torah, however, relentlessly attacks these deficiencies in order ultimately to make him *all* right — not in a manner of speaking, but in cold, hard reality.

This stark contrast demonstrates the Torah Jew's

whole approach to life. Everything that happens to him he views as a means used by Hashem to help him correct and refine his character. He is guided gently — and sometimes not so gently — not to hide from his inner self, not to make excuses for his misbehavior, not to rationalize away his mistakes. He knows that he is weak, inconsequential, and self-centered. But through learning Torah and doing mitzvot, he strives to make himself, with Hashem's help, a giver instead of a taker, a fully compassionate person instead of just a "nice guy," a self-sacrificing servant of Hashem instead of a servant of his own vain will and transient desires.

VII

THE KNOW-IT-ALL HUMAN MIND

An integral aspect of the successful western-culture man is his know-it-all attitude. His climb to the top is possible only if he believes that his independent power to decide what is right and wrong is superior and absolute. Nothing and nobody are really better than he, because such an admission would destroy his success image. Of course, the tactics of getting ahead may require a measure of modest submission to his superiors. And he can admit a lack of knowledge in areas outside his speciality (but, certainly, no lack of an opinion!). However, these gaps are only a matter of strategy or personal preference. He may listen to other people, but really *he* is the ultimate arbiter.

After all, his boss is this way: clear, decisive, uncompromising, driving through with his abilities until he shows everyone how right he is. Anyone seeing this model, much less working under it, would strive to be like it — if not for personal advancement, then at least for self-defense.

Even the many who accept that their understanding and abilities are limited adhere to a basic principle of western culture that a person must never be forced to accept anything that he does not understand or, by free will, agree with. Democracy requires the individual's prior approval. Given this huge power, the individual guards any infringement of his free will. "Nobody can tell me what to do!" He is boss over his own life, and nobody and nothing has any superior position over him.

This picture of independence is often revealed in all its shallowness. A whole variety of rules and responsibilities abridge his freedom of action. The tax collectors know all his financial moves. The policeman checks his driver's license. His boss demands endlessly, consuming whole chunks of his time and liberty. Home responsibilities have him running to the grocery or taking the children to school or playground. The electric bill is due and that important social gathering must be attended. Even his two-week vacation is not his own; where do the wife and children want to go and what about that long list of pending chores?

Still, he lives his image of knowing no master but his own free choice. In his mind and attitude, nothing is superior to him.

CONSTANT SUBJECTION

An individual can convince himself that he is independent, but if he looks at the situation honestly, he will realize that he is dependent. His original existence depended on Hashem giving him life, and his continued existence depends on Hashem continuing to give him life. He labors hard to make a living and excel in his work. But Hashem gives him the health so that he can work, and Hashem gives him the talent and brains to do his work well. Hashem brings in his clients and customers who will pay for his services. Hashem energizes and sustains the whole complex of forces that produce food, that connect the raw material to the finished product, that distribute and allocate resources, that bring to each man the full panoply of goods and services. Realistically, each individual is dependent on the smooth functioning of a huge interrelated system whose operation, like the operation of the universe itself, is totally dependent on Hashem.

The Torah Jew does not live these facts of his dependence just as an abstract thought. The daily requirements which Hashem puts on him in the form of mitzvot constantly work to make him realize his dependence on Hashem. He is obligated to do many things, regardless of his particular desire to do them. He must put on tefillin each morning; he must daven (pray) three times a day; he must give at least ten percent of his income to those in need; he must not turn on electricity on Shabbat; he must not contradict his parents; he must learn Torah even if he would rather do something else. In time, he will come to want to do many of the things which he is obligated to do. But there will always be things which he must do in spite of his personal desires in order to teach him the reality of his dependence and the concomitant necessity of his humbleness.

Torah, therefore, sharply challenges the western-culture image of independence. Torah teaches that Hashem built into man a feeling of independence because he was given freedom of choice — the one quality that makes him human and likens him to the Creator Himself. Western culture allows man to take this special gift and strut and roar until he has made himself supposed master over as much as he can. The Jew, through Torah and mitzvot, fights this natural inclination to imagine himself independent and, instead, intensifies his dependence on Hashem.

Through this process, he sensitizes himself to

his weaknesses, opening himself to a greater potential for perfection. He is not an animal that merely eats, sleeps, procreates and dies. He is a human being who has the free choice to rise above his animal nature. Further, by giving back to Hashem his freedom of choice, he shows that he understands where this capacity came from and for whose purposes it is to be used. If he used it only for himself, he would be like a child who does not let others use his toys, even the one who gave them to him. Instead, he recognizes that the test of life is whether he uses his freedom of action for his own purposes or for the purposes of Hashem; whether he traps himself (his free choice) within the limitations of finite existence ("what I want, I do") or frees himself (his free choice) to join a higher existence ("what the Source of Existence wants, I do").

If the individual dedicates his free choice to Hashem, the very element that could be set up in opposition to the Creator can be used to come closer to Him. Instead of asserting his independence, the Torah Jew concentrates on his dependence so as to convert his free will into a means of serving Hashem. He never lets his free will delude him into thinking himself important because then he would start in some degree to worship himself. Self-importance immediately blocks man's relationship with Hashem, who requires total adherence as the only means through which the created being can work his way back to the Source of his creation.

The mitzvot were designed by Hashem so that

every aspect of the human personality would be elevated to its highest plane by the free will of the individual accepting the Will of the Creator rather than following his own will. The brain is elevated through the study of Torah; the heart through prayer; the eyes through avoiding proscribed temptations; the ears through listening to the wisdom of the sages; the lips through the rules of proper speech — shunning foulness, gossip, derogatory language, lies; the stomach through kosher food; the arms through putting on tefillin; the body through modest clothing; the reproductive organs through *brit milah* (circumcision) and the laws of family purity; the human capacity to work and achieve through observing Shabbat; personal property through *tzedaka* (the rightful due of the needy) and spending on mitzvot.

As mentioned, Hashem created the human imperfect so that he would have the task in life of perfecting himself. Each means of perfection has already been prescribed in the Torah. The Torah Jew recognizes his imperfection and subordinates his free will to adopt what may go against his desires in order to follow a Higher Will. The more he accepts his dependence on Hashem, the more he can grow in his submission to His Will (Torah) and the more he perfects and elevates himself. He who asserts his independence avoids his weaknesses or tries to solve them through his own limited resources and ideas ("I want to do it my way!"). Ultimately he ends up little more improved than when he started and often frustrated and confused as to the purpose of his life and the real worth of his accomplishments.

The Torah Jew realizes that his dependence on Hashem must be total and complete. His mind is part of this dependence, and, therefore, when he does the mitzvot of Hashem he appreciates that he will not understand their full meaning because his mind — no matter how intelligent — is infinitely less capable than the Source that created this mind. Therefore, the Jew accepts that he cannot understand or know all the reasons. Indeed, part of the plan of the mitzvot is to teach the Jew that he does not know everything. Still, he is obligated to strive to achieve understanding, recognizing that understanding itself is a gift from Hashem. No person knows even how he came to be. So the Jew begins from this vantage point and joyfully admits his full dependence on the Creator and His Will. The person who pretends that he knows will never come to know. Whereas the Jew, who recognizes that he does not know, gradually through the Torah comes to know more and more each day.

VIII

THE DIFFICULTY OF FAITH

Ask the man on the street and he will tell you that reason is the province of science and the real world; faith is the business of clergymen and weak-willed people. And, obviously, he prefers the former, even though he may have faith that tomorrow will come, that his sport's team will vanquish the opponent, that the airplane in which he is flying will not crash, that the check which he just received in payment will be honored. Still, do not ask him to believe in too many angels and such.

The Jew in his assimilated western intellectual culture avoids contact with the concept of faith. Rather than adopt wishy-washy beliefs, he who has not been properly exposed to Torah will proclaim adherence to a code of "right conduct," based on practical, common-sense rules of humane behavior: don't lie, don't cheat, be nice to your neighbor, pay your bills, give the barber a tip . . .

Further, since beliefs have had the tendency to backfire on the Jew, he would prefer to have nothing to do with them. Sure, he believes in "country, mother and apple pie"; but these are general enough not to call for much commitment or attention. Moreover, the pluralistic society cannot involve itself too far in defining beliefs before it starts stepping on somebody's toes. So, better to stay distant and undefined.

Added to this social milieu is the intellectual-educated prejudice that disdains what seemingly cannot be examined analytically either through the academic-professional jargon or the laboratory test tube. "Religion," "belief," "faith" are just so much opinion, feeling and preference. What is "holy" to one is "profane" to another. Even health foods can become a religion! So, the whole subject either yields no worthwhile conclusions or is so beclouded in unmeaningful verbalisms that its relevance to the practical man's life is highly questionable. Besides, no one would consciously consider himself superstitious, and belief in things that deal with the supernatural borders on childish fantasy at best, ignorant foolishness at worst.

Any expression of spirit and faith that exists is often confined to the arts and literature, secularized and homogenized to a very low common denominator, indefinite enough to gain acceptance, yet specific enough to elicit some spiritual reaction. Thus, many yearn for a sense of peace within themselves and feel their connection with a "life force" that is energizing their existence. But they do not agree that these feelings are susceptible to an organized system of beliefs or prescribed behavior based on these beliefs. Whatever the person wants to do at any particular time is a satisfactory response to the moral and spiritual impulses which he personally decides are coming down from his conscience or from on high. Moreover, since belief is defined as something personal, everyone can plot his own course, and no one can or should interfere.

These types of belief, however, are vague and indefinite. People may believe that "life is basically good," "people are generally honest and considerate," "Hashem does exist up there," "peace will come when people respect one another," "happiness comes with being contented," "love conquers all." But these beliefs have little useful application to daily life. Maybe a person will smile more if he believes life worthwhile, but he will not change his impatience. Maybe he believes strongly in love, but he would not mind preempting a car parking-space. Maybe he believes in honesty, but adjusting his income-tax return is a different matter. There may be the bare bones of "faith," but the flesh of practical action is absent. Faith remains "in the sky" and is not a real part of life.

The Jew in western culture senses this paradox of the need for faith but the lack of a solid base. In general, he is idealistic, humanistic, optimistic, searching, open to exploring his full potential, serious, dedicated. But on what can he rest his faith? Organized religion has no appeal. Politics and democracy have been corrupted. Home and family have been disrupted by generation gaps and empty relationships. Professional and business successes are hollow, with no lasting satisfaction — just more rungs to climb. Even love is a bubble that can easily be burst for any one of a thousand reasons.

There is left the goal of making a better world: "if we conquer the unknowns of science"; "if we build housing projects for the poor"; "if we create more meaningful art"; "if we send everyone to college." In his need to sense faith, the Jew can sometimes spend his whole life pursuing these visions. Very often, the difficulty of the challenge and the necessities of a livelihood calcify these youthful dreams. And the small minority who fight on find their righteous causes making little impression on the society as a whole. Further, internally, they do not sense full contentment. After all, firemen can sleep some nights, but there is no real peace for those combatting everything.

The worst aspect of all these searchings for faith is that they have no system of nourishment, development or growth. Their form and direction are so amorphous that they remain in constant adolescence with no age of maturity. So people will say that they have no faith when in reality what faith they naturally had has simply atrophied from malnutrition. Or people will go around using a faith that is no more advanced than a child's view of the ice-cream man — ask and you will receive! And the unfortunate many staunchly believe that there is no such thing as spiritual faith *only* because they have not been exposed or educated in the nature and application of belief. They blindly say that belief in the Creator is a fictional crutch when all that they lack is a sensitizing of their inner awareness to see the reality of faith just as a tuned spectrometer can measure invisible electromagnetic waves. Light can exist in a vacuum; faith cannot.

JEWISH FAITH

Influenced by non-Jewish attitudes that faith is a blind adherence to the unknown, the sensible Jew is bound to reject faith. For this reason, Torah Judaism is particularly suited to his personality and potential. For it is not always possible to feel the exhilarating uplifts from contact with the spiritual forces which Hashem put into the human range of experience. And even if one does feel them, for how many minutes in the day can these "highs" be depended upon?

So Torah Judaism approaches faith from an entirely different side. The best way to learn a new language is to speak it. The best way to learn belief is to use it. How? Not by counting angels on pinheads, but by using the mind's grey matter to come to the deepest human understanding of reality. The Jew has belief because it is the *logical* outcome of his mental faculties applied to learning Torah—

Hashem's explanation to man of reality.

For example, the Torah teaches purity in sexual matters, humbleness at times of success, non-competitive concern for others, respect for old age and the wisdom of our sages, dedication to goals above our daily concerns, giving to others beyond our normal human tendency. The list is very long. And every Jew who is given the proper opportunity to learn Torah will see that for every life problem or issue there is a right Torah solution. "Right" — because in the most careful exercise of his intellect he is forced to agree that the Torah answer is truth.

So, what happens when he examines every issue in life through Torah analysis and finds Torah to be the only proper approach? He begins to reason quite logically that if Torah is right in this, in this, in this, in this, it must also be right in things that are not so readily comprehensible. Faith, then, becomes a by-product of a mind convinced that since everything else in Torah makes sense, when the Torah says to believe and have trust in the Creator, that too makes sense. Reason — clear, analytical brain power — buttresses and continually energizes the latent force in the Jew to believe.

Moreover, when one studies the Torah, one comes face to face with a thought process so magnificent in its depth, so challenging in its difficulty and so fulfilling in its total mental and emotional absorption that the individual and the Torah begin to form a bond. This bond lifts the individual not only above his normal mental capacities but also above the natural tendency to doubt that which is beyond the ordinary three dimensions and reaches the spiritual dimension. His faith becomes a factor of an entire human experience in which he is so amazed by all the greatness of what he is studying that he senses the Mind that is running everything. Once he tastes this realization, he does not doubt that the Torah is from Hashem, and he believes in Hashem and His constant activity in the world.

Beyond his own understanding that confirms his belief is the recognition that ultimately he cannot understand everything, a reality that gives true meaning to his belief. In learning something far greater than himself, the Jew is humbled to appreciate his true position in existence. Already he knows that he did not cause his own creation, nor can he prevent his physical end. Now, he sees that his mind — the most crucial element in his being — is overwhelmed by the breadth and complexity of Torah. His reaction is to admit his subservience and obeisance to the far higher Source, comprehending thereby that he, his mind and emotions are dependent functions of that higher Source. He builds his faith because he senses the cord that ties him beyond the realm of the physical to the realm of the spiritual. The Jew experiences this super-reality just as a man senses cold or happiness. It is real and it is truth. His faith is strengthened as a logical deduction from the greatness of what he is learning. The Mind that speaks to his mind through Torah is an Intellect that he can communicate with to the best of his ability. His own intellect brings him a positive awareness that Hashem exists, for he has labored with his brain to understand a higher level of thought and reality. He knows this dimension as well as he knows his own existence. Just as he knows the axioms of arithmetic, so also his mind comes to know the Oneness of Hashem's thought to the degree that man can appreciate it.

Moreover, this phenomenon occurs not only on an intellectual plane. Ever so gradually, he experiences an *emotional* involvement with the Torah which he is learning. His tasting of the intellectual pleasure affects his more subconscious system of feelings and character traits. The more he learns, the more he finds that his whole personality actually seeks complete identification with the Creator Himself. Because the words of Torah are from Hashem, the sincere student can re-create his unformed and imperfect self into the highest model possible for him — an *eved* (servant) of Hashem: someone who transcends his egocentricity and weaknesses to give himself completely back to the Source of his existence. In this dynamic process, he increases his belief because he becomes identified more and more with the object of his belief — Hashem. What was difficult to comprehend and accept now becomes more and more certain.

And this is no illusion, because the only way the next step in development can be made is if the last has become an integral part of his personality and behavior. (This process provides one explanation of why there are so many mitzvot: each mitzva has the potential to move the individual up in ever-increasing levels of human perfection, with the variety of mitzvot matching the variety of human personalities and levels.) Thus, if a person has done consistent acts of *chesed* (lovingkindness), increasingly more demanding ones will be within his capacity. For example, originally he gave only a small percentage of his income to Torah causes, but, as he keeps learning Torah and giving, he senses the need to give more and so he does. And if he tends to become angry easily, through the same process he can gradually control himself and not be provoked even where apparent justification exists.

As he sees himself changing, he begins to realize the power and effectiveness of his faith, and this faith, in turn, grows both intellectually and emotionally. His faith is not a rocking-chair passivity or a mere simple-minded, blind acceptance, but rather it is a dynamic maturing awareness of the greatness of the Creator and the interaction between Him and the individual, demanding active response and growth.

This process of authentic Jewish faith is not the only one for the Jew. Many Jews believe in Hashem and His Torah with a simple faith unclouded by questions or doubts. Actually, this is the higher form of faith which the process described above is geared to develop in the individual eventually. The Jew is supposed to act on his faith the way a millionaire writes a check. But many intellectual Jews and those estranged from Torah-Jewish patterns of living would reject the power of faith in their lives or would lack the confidence to use the kernel of faith which they do possess. Consequently they should realize that, contrary to general assumption, faith and belief are dynamic potentials of the Jewish personality, which can be diligently learned and realistically integrated into practical living. Just as no one would say that education about engineering or computers or medicine has no practical purpose, so, too, learning Torah has a practical result — the continual growth of trust in and reliance on Hashem. With this potent process of character improvement, a person can keep growing until he reaches the fullest closeness to the Creator that is possible for a human being. He will feel it, he will know it, he will be eager for more of it. Every day will be a fresh experience. Every day he will be able to climb higher.

Climbing this mountain of closeness to Hashem is exclusively a Jewish trip, a gift to the Jews from Hashem for His own purposes. And no greater challenge exists in the world. Whereas others may attempt the climb on an individual basis, adopting variations or imitations, only Torah Judaism is a total system, integrating belief and practice in order to achieve for a whole society a successful journey to the top. Judaism can claim this uniqueness not on its own merit but because Hashem in His kindness wants it this way, creating Torah and mitzvot and commanding the Jews to do the job of spiritually permeating the physical universe.* The Jew is no better than anyone else because "better" is a factor of potential and fulfillment of potential. That the Jew has a greater potential is undeniable — not so that he can become wealthy, but in order that he can complete the extremely difficult task which Hashem has given him. To complete this work he must use belief and faith, which grow in him as he grows. The more that he learns and lives Torah, the more he understands the spiritual force that is actually running life; the more he sees behind the veil of material existence and experiences for himself the Power that cannot be described, cannot be identified, and cannot even be imagined but, nevertheless, is. He senses it, he knows it, he lives it, and through the whole process his life becomes completely transformed and uplifted by it. *Every* Jew can do it if he is interested, becomes aware of the potential within him and actualizes that potential through following the Torah.

* To correct any erroneous implication that Hashem's selection was without basis, we note that the first Jew, Avraham, with his own understanding and insight realized the necessity of coming close to Hashem. (Each human being has this opportunity if he truly desires it.) Through Avraham's merit, we Jews have the task of continuing the life work which he started. And, indeed, when any Jew likewise comprehends the imperative to make Hashem manifest in his life and in the world, then he possesses and makes use of the legacy which he has inherited from his forefathers.

IX

LIFE MODELS

If one pauses to consider his life in western culture, he will be astounded to realize that there is almost no one around him whom he wants to be like. Sure, he likes this trait in one person, this quality in another. But on the scale of an *entire human personality*, no one is particularly appealing as a life model. This neighbor is a fine person and that college history professor is certainly upstanding. But these people do not lead the kind of lives that would prompt one to emulate them. Always, some weak or undesirable trait disqualifies any particular person from becoming the life pattern for any other individual.

As a result, the only models are composites of different people. One chooses certain qualities from various people and tries to combine them in himself in order to improve his own character and personality. This approach, however, is decidedly deficient. A strong relationship between the individual and any one of his models is unlikely, since having many models means that there is no one model with whom he can develop a close and influencing relationship. Further, there is no control over his development because no one figure exists whom he accepts and respects enough as his mentor and guide.

As a result, the individual remains alone — alone within the four walls of his own imperfections. Even so, he can remain content as he is because there is no one, in his opinion, really better than himself and no one in a position to prod him on to become a better person. Instead, with no real stimulus to improve and no inclination to seek out those who could urge his improvement, he sits rather helplessly amid poor traits and habits.

Of course, if he is a rising professional or businessman, he does adopt models of his success drive. Consciously or subconsciously, he imitates his boss or superior. His phraseology, mannerisms, and attitudes are all patterned to appeal to the man in charge of promotions, who himself stares at the hanging picture of the company founder. He who plays the drums sets the pace, and all who want to follow must march in time.

Such model-making is inadequate and even detrimental. Only part of the person's total character is being developed — the part that can make money. The inner workings of a human being — character traits, emotions, sensitivities — are left unattended and become atrophied. The individual becomes an automated robot of the system which he is plugged into. A banker thinks and behaves like a bank. A doctor thinks and behaves like a hospital. A lawyer thinks and behaves like a court. The molding process is gradual but inevitable, creating deformed, underdeveloped characters. In the absence of total life models, the partial ones fill the vacuum and absorb the individual's personality.

The individual does not even realize how he is being molded and manipulated. He thinks that he is being successful by imitating the higher-ups, but instead he is destroying himself. Why? Because the Jew was not born a scientist, a journalist, an engineer. He was born a Jew. To develop only his professional or work side neglects his totality — his Jewishness — which is tremendously larger than the subcategory of what he does to make a living. If he spends his life on developing only a part of himself, he has missed his once-in-a-lifetime opportunity to develop the whole of himself. In effect, he has wasted his life — a disastrous consequence of faulty and inadequate models.

But the overriding error in using the models of western culture is the acceptance of a man-made standard. For example, who decides what the perfect president is supposed to be like? Perhaps he himself does; perhaps Madison Avenue, the image makers; perhaps a synthesis of cultural values dependent on the time and place. A big smile is certainly a winner, and you can succeed without really trying if you are "in" with the boss. The real test of "right" is if it sells, if it is profitable, if it wins approval. Whether it is actually good is not the issue; if people think it is good, that is sufficient.

And what are the good models? A rich man, no matter how he climbed on others to get his riches. A smart man, no matter whether he is kind and considerate in his private life. A powerful man, no matter for whose benefit he uses his power. An attractive person, no matter how empty he is inside.

It is no wonder that young people reject the models of the older generation — man-made, fallible, impure, inconstant. A thinking person seeks something better, more perfect, more inspiring. But the Jew in western culture finds none that are acceptable.

THE TZADDIK

The Jewish model is the *tzaddik* (righteous person),
the completely perfect man as described in the
Torah. The Jew studies the Torah constantly and,
thereby, daily makes himself more like the model
delineated in the Torah. Seven fundamental qualities are epitomized in seven of the great Jewish
personalities, each possessing all of these qualities
but emphasizing a particular one in their lives:

Avraham — lovingkindness

Yitzchak — strict adherence to Law

Yaakov — the balance and harmony between
leniency and strictness

Moshe — humbleness (selfless identification
with the Eternal)

Aharon — the pursuit of peace

Yosef — the purity of the human body

David — the transformation of physical power
into spiritual energy

These seven pillars of the Jewish personality have been exemplified in thousands of Jewish lives down to the present age. Models of Jews working on human perfection have never been lacking. What has been lacking, unfortunately, are people interested in following these models. But the examples themselves have always existed and exist today: men and women who are purifying themselves to come closer and closer to Hashem.

Imagine a priceless masterpiece on display in a museum. It sits in a vacuum-sealed frame. A rope fence further protects it, and a guard is standing by. A special alarm system is connected and heavy locks secure the room. The museum itself is carefully closed and guarded at night. People flock to see the masterpiece, paying admission and studying it in depth. And all this effort is for an inanimate source of human elevation.

The Jewish human masterpiece is infinitely more priceless but far more accessible and, moreover, is instructive in the *total* human personality — not just beauty, but also kindness, discipline, intellect, selflessness. No locked doors or admission charges exist, but there is one important similarity. To avoid the harmful public light, the *tzaddik* cannot be studied out on the street. The humility which he is working on does not allow for fame and publicity. Delicateness and refinement require a certain hiddenness; otherwise, they can become spoiled. So, the Jewish model is often not readily apparent to the outsider or newcomer. But if he is truly seeking, he will find the model and stay close by in order to change himself and perhaps become, in turn, a model for others.

Every Jew has the potential to come closer to the examples of Jewish perfection. How close he approaches is a factor of his own interest and effort. Each is judged only according to the potential that he had to work with, and the task is every Jew's business, not just for a special few who are interested in "holy" things. Indeed, there is no other purpose to the Jew's existence except achieving the Jewish model of perfection. He was *not* born to become the best dentist, the best computer specialist, the best stockbroker. He was born to be the best *Jew*, a job infinitely more difficult because no ounce of energy and no second of time can be wasted. Every Jew paints a self-portrait during his life. Whether it is a masterpiece depends on whether he followed the model of a masterpiece — the *tzaddik*.

Where can these models be found? Within the Torah-Jewish environment there is no lack of proper examples to pattern one's behavior. Torah parents are the first and prime models, and they figure prominently throughout the Jew's life. Then come Torah teachers; and, finally, one's personal *rebbe* (teacher), with whom a strong relationship develops. Along with these, intensive Torah study shows us many more examples and teaches us how to integrate them into our behavior. Today, these life guides for character improvement are unknown to many Jews. But if they will understand:

(1) that such models are essential,

(2) that these models do exist, and

(3) that they must actively seek out these guides, then all this discussion about human perfection will yield for them the possibility of their own greater perfection.

X

RABBIS

Everyone knows who a rabbi is. He is the man who sits in the front of the synagogue, sermonizes for fifteen minutes during services (twenty on Yom Kippur), officiates at weddings and funerals, writes nice articles and can make off-the-cuff speeches with ease. He also is everyman's counselor, successful synagogue politician and community representative of the upstanding Jew.

In an age of specialization, the young Jew picks his profession: chemist, architect, professor, rabbi. The last has good pay and acceptable social standing; so if he likes that "religious" stuff, then, okay, he can be a rabbi.

Today, the rabbi stands between the older people who are comfortable with the way things have been run and the young people who are interested in making changes. The older ones carry more weight, but the rabbi feels a need to attract those who are

91

not as yet part of the establishment. And certainly they have a point: unintelligible and boring services should be changed. Judaism must be "relevant," like theater-in-the-round, group therapy, and musical happenings!

Still, to keep his job, the rabbi must master the art of compromise. As with other diplomats, what he actually stands for is less important than that he appears to stand for something. And if he has succeeded in making nearly everyone his friend (or at least the synagogue governing board), he has reached the highest rung of accomplishment. His position is secure and his congregants are happy.

It is no wonder, then, that such a rabbi, even when he is sincere in his efforts, is not considered a model or guide to the Jews who know him. The older ones do not expect or desire such a role; so the rabbi has not disappointed them. But, for the younger Jews, he could have fulfilled their guidance needs, but he is too compromised, under-trained and pre-occupied with a hundred functions. Besides, even if his advice is sought, he must compete with the family lawyer, doctor and psychologist. True, at least he is on the list. But nobody imagines that he is any more aware, wise or capable than anyone else in society. After all, "rabbi" is a job classification, an artful speaker, a functionary at weddings ...

THE TORAH RAV

The term "rabbi," like the term "Judaism," has been so twisted out of shape that neither is useful without further definition. We have tried to explain that "Torah Judaism" is the one-hundred-percent commitment to follow the will of the Creator as He expressed it unalterably to the Jewish People through Moshe Rabbenu (our teacher) at Har Sinai 3300 years ago. Other forms of so-called Judaism may use the word but are only parts or alterations of the original, permanent version. The label is a misnomer if it means anything other than the authentic, immutable tradition.

"Rabbi" can mean someone who has passed a certain number of college-level courses and received a diploma saying that he is now a "rabbi." He can be someone who turns on electricity on Shabbat, eats non-kosher meat and does not wear a *kippa* (head covering). It can even be someone who does not believe in Hashem. All these are misusing the term if they call themselves "rabbi."

The title "rabbi" in Torah Judaism is quite specific: a man learned in the Law of the Torah and who abides by that Law. Ideally, every male Jew should be a rabbi because every Jew is obligated to be learned in the Law of the Torah and to observe that Law. Some do not have the intellectual capacity to be learned. But every Jew who is gifted with sufficient intelligence is *required* to be a rav (rabbi).

It is not by accident that the basis of every social system is law, the means by which life is regulated and ordered. As mentioned, the law of nature rules the non-human world; the Law of the Torah governs the human world. Hashem commanded both laws for the maximum performance of both systems. The Jew who senses his Jewishness realizes that his optimum functioning depends on his knowing the Law that orders his existence. In the process of learning how life should properly be lived, the Jew becomes a rav, i.e., someone learned in Torah. Whether he ever uses his knowledge to make a livelihood is entirely a secondary issue. In the Torah-Jewish culture, where everyone is learned, only the most outstanding take on the roles of unofficial or official leaders. Only in an age where Torah learning has failed to reach the large body of the Jewish People is a "rabbi" considered a livelihood rather than the societal paradigm of the human striving for perfection.

The degree to which a Torah-Jewish rav is respected and honored would amaze the uninitiated Jew. The great ones are considered the pillars upon which the world continues to exist. Their rulings are followed implicitly; their wisdom is circulated and preserved for all to learn; their deeds are eternally revered. In each generation many such men exist. But they are known only in the circles that are interested in knowing them. As discussed, publicity is counter to the humility which is inherent in their greatness, and their power is lost in an environment uninterested in or even hostile to the values which they represent. But the Jew who is seeking such life models can find them.

Man's having been created in the image of Hashem is a basic Torah principle. It means that he is expected to imitate the qualities of Hashem to the best of his ability. Torah teaches the characteristics of Hashem and how to emulate them. The rav who has learned Torah over many decades and has made his learning part of his life epitomizes the closest model to human perfection that exists on this earth. The Jew who is on a lower level of human perfection can raise his level by associating with, learning from, and patterning himself after a rav. This model becomes a real-life means of improving the standard of his human conduct. By this process he, too, develops the image of Hashem in which he was created and with which he can come closer to Hashem Himself. Then he also becomes a rav and helps others in turn.

XI

PARENTS

Western culture is particularly pleased with the image of parents which it has created: father knows best and mother cooks best. The ideal parents are a mixture of all the choicest ingredients: wisdom, patience, love, understanding, giving, kindness, stability, guidance, friendliness, sacrificing. You name it, they have it.

Under such demanding standards, it is no surprise that the image is paper-thin and the reality has become a near fiasco. True, Jewish parents are rated highly in many categories: the qualities of giving, responsibility, concern. But they are not their children's models for how to live and view life. Indeed, it is seldom that the two generations communicate on a meaningful plane. Father has his values, and son, his own values; mother is involved in her activities, and daughter, hers. Father emphasizes financial security; son yearns for creativity.

Mother is concerned about public appearance; daughter seeks out the unconventional. Son learned "new math" and father still uses the old formulas. Daughter is a free spirit who prefers no attachments, and mother encourages settling down. The proverbial ships passing in the fog may be an adequate metaphor of the relationships.

There is disagreement in so many different areas of life that conversations are often debates: politics, economics, the status of the under-privileged, raising the grandchildren, use of leisure time, the approach to life and solving its problems. The lines are often so fixed that further discussion is unnecessary. And why?

One reason is the march of "progress." If everything is getting more modern, then the older generation is not as up-to-date as the new generation. The new generation can justifiably claim that decisions cannot be made on the basis of past experiences because "things have changed." As a result, parents are no longer competent to guide their children because they have become obsolescent, a model from a previous year no longer in style.

Such attitudes also reflect a shallowness in their association. Little time is used to develop meaningful ties between the generations. Each is busy in his own world with few interactions. Furthermore, the time spent together is minimal and kept neutral — first, because of the differences and, second, because of the impersonality of the activities. Entertainments, sports, traveling — all occupy the individual with an object but rarely with another person. Depth in personal relationships cannot be cultivated while the television set is playing. Nor will the pleasures of a ski lodge or a classical concert or a hard game of tennis open new insights between people.

Some parents create a relationship by becoming "pals" with their children. The parent adopts the values and mores of his child in order to gain acceptance. Communication is salvaged because the parent agrees with the new generation and tries to behave like it. Of course, this approach removes the parent as a model for the child because, in effect, the reverse has happened.

The undercutting of the older generation's position by "progress" and by becoming "pals" has left the younger generation adrift and without meaningful guidance. The result has been a grand trek in search of models — to India, to Tibet, to Europe, to the western United States. Additionally, since they have little in common with their parents, the children feel no particular need to live near them. Distance preserves non-interference and freedom of action, avoiding the problems of the differing viewpoints and value systems.

This hopeless situation is also a logical result of a principle discussed earlier. In a culture with no definite standards and everything relative to individual desire, parents cannot represent the model of the proper life-style since this element is postulated as a variable with which the next generation can readily disagree. So, except for various general values (e.g., work hard, stay straight), parents stand for very little. They claim no truth, but the younger generation is seeking truth, and so it must perforce look and live elsewhere.

TORAH PARENTS

As explained, the Torah Jew stands opposed to the relativism and lack of absolute truth in western culture. Instead, he lives and represents a set code of behavior for every particular in life, with each rule specially designed by Hashem to elevate him to a higher level of human completeness.

Since the parent typifies the highest of human aspirations within a clear pattern of daily living, the children see and live with a model beyond compare. They are thus able to learn not only standards of behavior but also how to actualize these standards through hard work and vigorous honesty. Their own striving for truth and perfection is answered in their parents' striving for truth and perfection.

As the children grow and become independent, they find that they have more in common with their parents, not less. When young, they are obviously being directed and guided very closely. But as they mature in thought and emotions, the children must on their own resolve their approach to life. No one is a robot, least of all Jews! Through their own learning of Torah and through seeing it practiced by their parents, the children discover that their innermost needs are fulfilled through the very way of life which their parents are leading. They respect and admire their parents because they epitomize the process of seeking perfection which they themselves consider the task of life. Indeed, the parent realizes that, even though he is the first and prime model for the child, higher-level guides are needed. So he sends the child to the very best Torah teacher in order that the child can continually grow. The child may even develop greater awareness than his parent, but because his way of life is exactly the same as his parent's, the unity of purpose and appreciation of common values intensify the bond between the two generations. The second generation is a continuation of the first and so on to grandchildren, great-grandchildren, great-great-grandchildren.

Because these values (closeness to Hashem and human perfection) and the means to achieve them (the mitzvot) are above the vicissitudes of time, in no generation are they subject to change or alteration. What is above time and place cannot be affected by those in time and place. Therefore, the new generation is only too eager to carry forward the weighty responsibility of fulfilling the same high objectives and work of the previous generation.

Such unity of purpose creates a meaningful, concerned and unending relationship. Parents have an active and direct role in educating their children from youth through adulthood. The father studies the same material that his son studies. Indeed, they learn *together* the same Gemara, the father imparting his accumulated knowledge and wisdom and the son adding his own unique insights. The mother trains the daughter in running a household and helps her once she is married and has children of her own. The father teaches the son how to put on tefillin and how to daven. The mother shows the daughter how to kasher the meat and take *challa* (required portion of dough) from the bread she bakes. Shabbat and the festivals are family affairs, constantly infusing the relationships with shared joy and happiness. Parents activate their responsibility to guide their children; the children express their gratitude for all they have received from their parents by helping them in every way, particularly when old age makes the parents dependent on the child for personal care and attention. Parents and children develop strong bonds and are united in attitude and affection. Instead of living far from their parents, the children prefer to live close by. Instead of avoiding parents' advice, the children seek it out. Instead of challenging the life-style of their parents, the children endeavor wholeheartedly to follow it.

Opposed to the western-culture view that life is various parts and independent units, Torah Judaism sees life as a whole, as one unit—a manifestation of the Oneness of Hashem. A parent and a child are not separate units, each going about his own business. Nor is this relationship a detachable portion of life which, if unfulfilled, may contentedly be skipped over or replaced by some other activity.

Nor is it by accident that life is based on the parent-child pattern. This structure is no artificial imposition on human freedom. The parent-child relationship is a learning tool for achieving the Hashem-human relationship.

The child receives from the parent life, sustenance, shelter and affection and is guided and disciplined by him. The child's gratitude and obedience to his parents are basic traits that lead him to appreciate the kindnesses which he is receiving constantly from Hashem and to respond by obeying His commandments. In his youth, he may imagine his parents to be all-powerful, an illusion dissipated with time. But Torah parents immediately teach the child that what he receives is coming not from them but *through* them from Hashem. As the child matures, he appreciates that his parents are the agents of the Father that created him and them too. As he senses and fulfills his responsibilities to his parents, he realizes that he has responsibilities to a higher Source. In feeling his parents' protecting and disciplining hand, the child is preparing for the day when the hand of Hashem will be more directly guiding him. Thus, the parent-child relationship prepares him for his adulthood and is a necessary building block in his achieving greater knowledge of the way in which Hashem works in the world.

The analogy works on the parent as well. He (who helped to create) experiences the outflowing of love for his child (the one created). The compassion and concern which he feels for his offspring help him to understand how Hashem feels for him. He sees a bit more clearly the tremendous love that Hashem shines upon the world, and this realization encourages him to respond with more kindness and giving.

Through the requirement to lead the child on the proper path, the parent understands the absolute necessity for a rule-system of right conduct for adults as well. Further, even if in ignorance the child objects and feels temporarily hurt or abandoned because of discipline and punishment, the parent knows that love is his motivation. Thus, the rewards and punishments of Hashem are somewhat less of a mystery to him.

In sum, the Torah parent-child pattern is an antidote to the western culture's situation. Instead of losing influence over the children as they mature, the Torah parent gains even greater respect because the children better appreciate the model which the parent represents, a model of complete dedication to the will of the Creator. Indeed, the children are inspired to imitate their parents' high spiritual and moral goals, unadulterated by materialism, self-indulgence and vanity. The parent is not just a friend or occasional advice-giver. He is the prime example to the child of how to live. The child's first reaction to any situation is to ask what would be his parents' approach to the problem. Likewise, he would never do anything to violate intentionally the will of his parents. Just as they have humbled themselves before the will of Hashem, so too the child learns humility before them in order ultimately to humble himself before Hashem.

The parent also learns under Torah that the child is not his private property. On the contrary, Hashem owns everything, and the Jew holds only temporary leases which are subject to Torah provisos. The relationship, therefore, is less apt to make the child a forced alter ego of the parent. A prime purpose of the Torah life-style is to convert private, egoistic desires into a pure will to serve the Creator. Everything that the parent makes the child do, therefore, should be based on Torah, thereby removing private motivations and unconscious ego drives. The child respects a parent who does not act arbitrarily but who exercises his power consistent with a higher Authority. Such an approach yields mutual respect, concern and consideration, where parent and child interact and join forces to serve Hashem. The cornerstone of this process is Torah and the fervent desire of parent and child to fulfill it.

XII

EDUCATION

In western culture, education is, like other areas of life, specialized and neutralized. The specialization leaves the job to a select few, parents not included; and the neutralization neglects the individual's character improvement since there is no one right moral system. The educational system works on the person's outer mechanics, his intellect, his skills and talents, but never touches his inner motivations — goals, purposes, emotions, search for meaning. Education is viewed as a means of fulfilling one's economic-producing potential and only tangentially of worth for its own sake. Education's professionals — the academics — are specialists and technicians but rarely life models or examples of human perfection. The educational system is impersonal, inanimate and unresponsive. Motivation is instilled coercively and artificially. Most of what is learned is mastered for examination and forgotten. While the competitive system already prepares the student for the future, it corrupts emotions and destroys relationships. Time is wasted and inefficiently used. The social environment undermines the supposed seriousness of the entire venture. And, finally, the system stops when the person is still young, indicating that the real bulk of life's learning is elsewhere. And if formal education is returned to later, it is generally at the individual's discretion, showing that it is unrequired and unessential. This disparaging synopsis requires some elaboration.

Education is valued because it leads to the central goals of society — money and prestige. Early in life, a person must think about what he is going to be, how will he make a living. This purpose molds the course of his education — training to become a producing unit of society. Nowhere along the line is he told what the purpose of all this production is. The answer is left to his own imagination and decision.

But, in the meantime, the schools and universities achieve their role of preparing for the next step in life — how to make money. This system, however, does not seek to guide or assist the student to understand what is the purpose of life and what is his role within that purpose. The teachers are simply not concerned with the answers to such questions. Indeed, the silence is so pervading that one would think that the issues do not even exist! Pluralistic, democratic society leaves such problems for the individual privately to resolve. So the huge bulk of time within the educational labyrinth is completely devoid of meaningful guidance on basic issues.

Of course, the parents think that their children are receiving a proper education. The "specialists" are handling the problem, and parents accept their lack of background and training in the new knowledge of the day and pedagogical techniques. Further, their own busy roles in modern specialized society give them little time to devote to their children. The schools, however, never claim to be the total educators, admitting that the home is where the child should learn basic morals, values and proper behavior. "Purpose in life is not our business to teach," they say. And so the child falls through the gap in the middle, as each side tosses the responsibility to the other.

The results of this "buck-passing" are now at disaster levels. There is ever-decreasing respect for authority. Indeed, discipline problems make the actual teaching almost a secondary activity. Students are confused and bewildered, dissatisfied with learning dry facts that bring no meaning to their lives. So, they search for every new experience imaginable in order to find meaning: drugs, meditation cults, communes, violence gangs, gurus, eastern religions. Jewish parents who never dreamed that the term "juvenile delinquents" would be applied to their children now pay lawyers, doctors, social workers, psychologists, and psychiatrists to extricate their children from the results of incomplete education and inadequate guidance at home and in school.

It is an amazing reality of western education that, after the first few grades of elementary schooling, where the needs of social integration require inculcating rules of conduct, no serious effort is employed to improve moral and ethical behavior. Indeed, one could say the opposite: behavior patterns reach a lowest common denominator where competition yields to cheating on examinations and papers; where co-education reduces decorum through clothes preoccupation, flirting, dating and illicit relations; where mechanized mass education produces people who can operate like machines but who have little concern for or interest in their fellow human beings.

Somehow, the few concepts of right and wrong picked up in passing are supposed to serve the individual in the myriad of complex personal relationships and responsibilities — including even the whole fabric of legal obligations imposed by secular law. The only time the average individual seriously learns any law is when he applies for his driver's license. The educational system exists to train people how to live and leaves the law — the basis of the society's system of living — to those few who want to specialize in that field. How does anyone claim to be law-abiding?

Indeed, everyone ends up as a specialist devoted to maintaining one part of the societal vehicle. He does not know what the purpose of the vehicle is nor where it is going. He may not care if other parts break down so long as his section is functioning. And like the mechanism itself, he works on the outward results and pays little or no attention to what is going on inside. If things are moving along (gas in the tank and money in the pocket), everything must be all right.

But the surest indictment of the educational system is that it applies only to certain categories: children, young adults, those interested in job advancement and those with spare time and curiosity. The great bulk of the adult society is completely outside the educational system. Indeed, this mass of people demonstrate by such behavior that further knowledge for them is unnecessary since, apparently, they know all that they need to know. Certainly, they study professional literature to maintain their living, read the newspapers to keep up with what is happening and skim the best sellers to make intelligent conversation. But for them, life has no new horizons of knowledge or intellectual endeavor. What they learned when they were just achieving full maturity and before is enough education for them. Now there is no need and no time for more; making an income and having a good time are sufficient.

How can it be that an adult does not continually need more education? Does he stop filling his stomach when he reaches the age of twenty-five so that he could reason that he no longer has to fill his brain? Did the process of education which he absorbed when young so inspire him that now he has no interest in further learning? Does the race for money and prestige so involve his energies that there is no opportunity to develop whole caverns of undiscovered potentials and awarenesses yet within him? When he thinks of more education, does he remember lifeless lectures, boring and irrelevant fact compilations, grand theories and philosophies with no meaningful application? Has he so refined and perfected the totality of his personality and character that there is nothing more anyone can teach him, nothing more that needs improvement?

TORAH EDUCATION

Recalling the purpose of a Jew's life, we can understand what education means in the Torah culture. The Torah Jew is required to perfect his intellect and behavior to approach the absolute perfection of Hashem. To accomplish this demanding obligation, he studies the thoughts of Hashem in His Instruction Book, the Torah. Since these thoughts have the potential to elevate the individual to the highest level of pure intellect and moral behavior that he is capable of, the Jew learns Torah the *whole* of his life, *every day* of his life.

Obviously, then, Torah education is totally different from secular education. Torah learning begins when the child utters his first word and ends when, on his death bed, the Jew utters his last word. It totally absorbs his mind and activity, leaving him with no extra time except for necessities. He listens to the words of his rabbis as if his life depended on each word. He is stimulated by every subject because it relates to him in a personal way, because each word of Torah comes to help him achieve his fullest perfection. During his learning, he is uplifted by Torah's purity, sublimity and power to change his life for the better. The more he learns, the more he wants to learn. The deeper he understands, the more he thirsts for even more profound understanding.

What he learns he puts into practice. Theory is constantly applied to the practical: he learns about the mitzvot and does them. Hashem continually tests him to make certain that what he is learning has become a part of his growth. Just as his mental capacity expands under the constant effort to comprehend extremely intricate reasoning, so too his heart and emotions grow in their sensitivity to the spiritual dimension of life since the ultimate Intellect is also the ultimate Spirit. He begins to know Hashem, so to speak, as his mind begins to appreciate ultimate Intellect, being both challenged and humbled to yield his imagined superiority to that which is truly superior. The more he studies and uses what he studies, the more he raises himself above his former level of behavior and achieves greater and greater levels of purification in character, personality and thought.

So one sees that Torah education is cast in a powerful mold. Diligent persistence and complete dedication are necessary from the very beginning to the very end. A child is trained and guided from the *Aleph-Bet* to *Chumash* (Pentateuch) to Mishna to Gemara. Strong supervision is directed from the home, with the father primarily responsible for the son's progress and the mother for the daughter's. There is no split between what is learned in school and what is practiced at home. The teacher is the direct agent of the parent, and the parent is obliged to supplement substantially the teacher's efforts by teaching the subject matter as well or, at the very least, testing the child *weekly* on his progress. Indeed, the same thing the child is learning, the father is also learning, though at a higher level. The Torah father realizes that just as the sacred learning and observances were carefully and perseveringly passed on to him from his parents and the generations before, so also must he fulfill his responsibility of successfully passing them on to his children. Not because venerable customs are pleasant to keep around. No, absolutely not! Torah education from generation to generation is the *life link* from the original giving of Torah at Har Sinai to the present time. This gift is so precious and so extraordinary that it is the *only* thing that makes life worthwhile. With no other behavior or thought system in the world can a Jew create spirit from matter, releasing the eternal sparks within himself and his environment and distilling from the finite its essence of infinite.

It is no wonder, then, that the Jewish child is educated to say *berachot* (blessings) as soon as he can talk; that at age three or four he is sent to preschool classes where he learns the basics of the *Aleph-Bet* and initial vocabulary; that at five to seven he enters into the richness of the Chumash and Mishna, already learning in school from morning to late afternoon, with no long summer vacations. And by eight or nine, he is learning Gemara, which is so complex that it can totally challenge a man in his full maturity and mental strength. This rigorous intensity during childhood is essential if the proper foundation is to be built for successful learning throughout the Jew's life. (It is no wonder, then, that the Torah-educated child's bar mitzva at the required age of thirteen is a meaningful and growing experience and not a mere excuse for an extravagant party.)

One can readily see that the Jew learns not because he has nothing better to do or merely because the subject is interesting or fascinating. He learns because it is the *only* way he has to correct, perfect and purify himself. Since he must reach his optimum before the time when he gives up his body and his *neshama* (soul) returns to its Source, no time can be wasted and every moment possible is used to learn. His mind stays fresh, alert and growing all the way to the end. Not for him is an old age of puttering around in the garden or dozing in the armchair opposite the television. Instead, he now taps the vintage of a lifetime of human development and strives ever further.

The learning itself is the task of the Jew because that is what Hashem wants him to do: devote all his mental and emotional energies to serve Him — not in any way we might think is a good way to serve Him, but the way *He* thinks is a good way. In this manner, the Torah Jew learns the most essential lesson of all: his subservience to the will of the Creator. Just as his next breath of air depends on Hashem's will, so also his intellect and behavior must depend on Hashem's will. Thus, he takes his independent will and gives it back to Hashem. How? By constantly learning how his will should be used. As soon as the Jew imagines himself free to do what he wants, he is making a mistake. Only when he continually learns what Hashem wants (Torah) will he curb his false sense of independence, reduce his tendency to err and eventually come to do more of what is truly pure and right. For this mission he needs education, Torah education.

XIII

THE WORLD OF PARTS

The entire unhealthy nature of western culture has become a blatant reality. And we are not just referring to the air pollution, noise pollution, insecticides, mercury poisoning, food preservatives. There is no whole, only parts; and everyone feels disconnected and unjoined. Even apart from the boom in the psychiatry and psychology business, the shredding of the mental structure of society is apparent. Alcohol and drugs have become ways to cope with the meaninglessness of life. The whole life-style skates on the surface most, if not all, of the day, with formal, routine or uninvolved interactions at home, on the subway, in the office, in the stores and shopping centers.

Escaping into entertainments — television, pleasure reading, travel — is an open attempt to shut oneself off from the outside world and be content, avoiding serious issues or life problems. Sinking oneself into one's work or profession, as well as developing absorbing hobbies and sports, are also means of hiding from oneself. The expectation is that by developing his skills a man can find himself. But in this determined effort he finds only the part that he is working on so hard. He may be a successful contractor, accountant, optician, but the rest of him (maybe 75% or more) is crying out for development, satisfaction and meaning. He has become an excellent technician, but, like the part he is working on, he feels fragmented, incomplete and lacking a sense of the whole. Of course, the culture has developed coping mechanisms, such as professional organizations to institutionalize one's identity, the drive for success to utilize all one's time, vacations, table tennis, piped-in music, and a thousand other escapes. But, in sum, the whole structure is a skyscraper built on sand and steadily sinking in.

WHOLENESS

The Jew's absorption in learning Torah and doing mitzvot is the complete reverse of the "world of parts." Torah and mitzvot deal with the totality of human existence. For the unity of Hashem is reflected in the unity of His Torah, so that every detail of human thought, emotion and activity is covered. The One who created everything revealed the relationship of each part to the others and the necessary behavior required to achieve the maximum fusion. The Designer knows how the whole mechanism fits together, how harmony exists among the multitude of parts. Man, who comes into the world incomplete, has been given the challenge of creating harmony within himself and his environment. His manual is the Torah, and, when put into sincere and diligent operation, it yields completeness and wholeness.

For if we analyze the "world of parts," the

misery derives from a failure to comprehend or even to envision the whole. Each person is in his own dinghy, bobbing around and seeing water as far as the horizon. He may even be an expert in his department, but inside he feels no wholeness, no harmony, no real understanding. Not so for the Torah Jew who follows his heritage.

Torah describes how to get up in the morning and how to go to sleep at night. It tells one how to make a living. It prescribes proper conduct between parents and children, husband and wife, teacher and student, customer and storekeeper. Food, clothing, utensils, festivities, mourning, marriage, how to meet crises, what to do with every minute of the day, how to help others, how to uncover the inner self, how to mature, how to become less selfish and egocentric — everything is included. And the perceptive student of life jumps to alertness as he appreciates more and more how every part of life can become an integral whole, how he can regulate his life so that it will function in perfect rhythm and harmony.

Most people are fascinated by well-functioning physical systems — a jumbo jet, an electronic watch, an automobile, the human body — in which each part works smoothly with the others. Yet they ignore the proper functioning of their own spiritual-mental-emotional system. They limp along on one piston, so to speak, content that they are moving, though subconsciously aware that power and drive are missing. Since everybody else is moving with about the same diminished capacity, they pass it off and imagine that the mechanism is functioning normally.

Torah does not allow a person to fool himself that he is operating at peak efficiency. On the contrary, Torah constantly pushes for better performance. Since "there is nothing new under the sun," life's situations have been standard since the beginning of time: love, hate, jealousy, lust, greed, pettiness. The external coatings may be altered to suit changing styles, but the principles stand immutable. Does a man lose his temper or not? Does he use illegal means to become rich or not? Does he give in to his lusts or not? Does he rely on his physical possessions for security or not?

Torah knows all these tests, teaches them to the Jew, and prepares him to pass them. How? By (1) training his mind to work in a controlled and disciplined manner so that he will not yield to his weaker side; and (2) training his heart to appreciate fully his absolute dependence on Hashem so that pride in his mind will not lead him to use it as an injurious weapon of private power. The first comes through constantly studying Torah, which teaches analytical reasoning, deep concentration power, mastery of the most difficult concepts, a huge compendium of knowledge in the natural sciences, liberal arts and social sciences. The second comes through doing mitzvot, the prescribed actions which continually subject the ego to Hashem. So, for example, the Jew wears a garment with *tzitzit* (knotted cord) on the corners which he can see to remind him that he is bound to an entire system of behavior (the mitzvot) which the Creator requires him to obey. He puts on tefillin, binding his arm and head with *battim* (compartments with Torah inscriptions) and straps in order to subject all his physical and mental powers to the service of the Creator and not use them merely for his own private gratification. He prays three times a day at prescribed times with a prescribed text to realize that he has to check in with the "Boss" every so often.

These examples are just three of many means which Hashem devised so that each Jew can correct the faults within himself. We must do *each and every one* of them because otherwise we would naturally do what comes easiest and avoid the mitzvot in areas where our character is weak. Moreover, the whole process of learning Torah and doing mitzvot lifts us above our ordinary physical limitations because once we have demonstrated a humble concern to do the will of the Creator, He assists us even more to overcome life's tests and challenges. The Jew has only to desire to come close to Hashem, and Hashem helps him. This process combats the "world of parts." The Torah Jew gains meaning in life; he directs his energies positively and selflessly; he senses harmony within life's many contending forces; he tastes the beauty and joy of spiritual experiences; he perceives more and more the whole of existence, the Creator Himself.

XIV

FREEDOM — WESTERN STYLE

Such close control of the Torah Jew's activities is in strong opposition to the principle of western culture that the individual is free to run his life the way he wants. To regulate clothes, hair, food, marriage, learning, making a living and money is viewed as a sign of antiquated regimentation that destroys the free human spirit and leads to a dull, unimaginative life. Further, to adopt such a complete form of regulated behavior — especially one based on ancient principles — is not rational for a free-willed, intelligent human being. Why should he give up his freedom of choice and put himself in a straightjacket? Better to be free to do as he pleases.

We have already discussed what western-culture freedom means as a practical matter: so many responsibilities and obligations that the individual has not a moment of his own — job, family, mortgage, taxes, household chores, community affairs, necessary relaxation. His big vacation time is a valiant effort to change his whole environment so that he can forget how patterned and regulated he is. So off he travels to the mountains, the seashore or a foreign country to find that he must maneuver within little time and a tight schedule during his one period of "freedom." And still, somehow, he imagines that others live in a strait-jacket, but not he.

Also mentioned was the degree to which people try to develop themselves, using their freedom of action and creativity in their work. But a job or profession is just a part of the Jew. Unfortunately, because of western culture, he can sink himself into his occupation without tapping his full Jewish potential and purpose, missing his main reason for being.

Many, of course, crave to use their free time to experience other things in life besides their work. Nearly everything they do, though, leaves them much the same when they finished as when they started. A dramatic novel is remembered until the press of important activities. A vigorous ball game releases body tension for a while. A ceramic artfully designed, a sailboat built and navigated, a dress gracefully sewn — all contribute to a sense of accomplishment. But when we look over time at the inner core of the individual, we see little permanent change in character or personality development, nor has he raised his human dimension above the physical.

The situation has become so stagnant and un-creative that a whole anti-societal subculture has developed, which rejects the bourgeois norms and patterned existence of western-culture man. These people want to be free, and to them wearing a pin-striped, three-piece suit with accompanying attaché case resembles a uniform — a prison uniform. Thus, freedom is created through non-customary behavior: long hair, dungarees, disdain of social amenities and convention, particularly the 9-to-5 job and the family structure. They feel themselves free because they reduce to the absolute minimum what they are required to do, postulating that if the individual does what he wants when, where and how he wants, then he must be free.

Observing the "free" culture according to its claims, we see that it fails in its hopes. The dunga-rees and long hair become a uniform in themselves. Their position is fixed, and they become as im-movable in their viewpoint as the middle-class suburbanite. Indeed, their "freedom" prevents them from changing or developing other ways of living.

Even more fundamentally erroneous is their basic concept of freedom. Freedom implies choice, i.e., there must be two sides to an issue before one is free to decide. If the anti-culture people condition themselves to do whatever they want whenever they want, they develop a pattern without limits or controls. Their actions are no longer free since their personal desires control and dictate their lives. The individual becomes enslaved to his impulses, losing the freedom of choice to say "no" to his own wants. He is not in control; his desires are.

This basic error reveals the face behind the mask: the anti-culture groups epitomize western culture's first principle: that the individual is number one. Whereas western culture merely believes this axiom, the subcultures live it. Obviously, then, as discussed, when number one is the person himself, he has lost the freedom and potential to move above the finite confines of his own existence and to come closer to the true Number One.

TORAH FREEDOM

The Torah Jew's test of freedom is not how much he does what *he* wants, but how much he does what *Hashem* wants. Since he was created by Hashem, Hashem knows best how he can fulfill his being. The manufacturer knows best how his product should work. The personal desires and wants of the individual can block his optimum development because they are manifestations of his own limited understanding and strong personal biases. Being subjective about himself, he can rarely make an objective decision — a decision more accurate and necessarily of greater benefit to him. Constantly misjudging the situation to some degree, he can become chained to his own misconceptions. Many people are very happy to live this way, insisting that they would rather do their own "thing" and be wrong than to adopt what may be truth but which is imposed. So their being "free" maintains them in a position subservient to their erring minds.

The Torah Jew, on the other hand, devotes himself as much as he possibly can to following the will of the Creator and avoiding the pitfalls of his faulty mind and viewpoints. The absolute truth of Torah, transmitted by Hashem-fearing rabbis, provides an objective guide to all of life's problems and difficulties. The Torah Jew thereby avoids being bound within his subjective and error-prone decision-making. He gives up his freedom to make mistakes and be wrapped up in himself in order to be elevated to the freedom of right conduct. In a classic paradox, he — by giving up his freedom — becomes free. By renouncing the supremacy of himself and accepting Hashem's supremacy (through Torah and mitzvot, as explained), he breaks the bonds of his own limitations and takes on the potential of limitlessness, i.e., the freedom to achieve his absolute best all of the time. Now he is truly free because he is no longer subject to the weaknesses of his character and personality. Instead of giving into these faults, he triumphs over them, extricating himself from their destructive hold and releasing latent qualities of purer human good and perfection. For the end result which he achieves, he is more than willing to trade a momentary impulse to exercise his personal wishes for a lasting improvement in the quality of his life by following Hashem's will.

Life requires choices, and choices perforce delimit freedom. If one wants to become an engineer, he has to limit his freedom to do other things while studying engineering. If one wants to read a book, he withdraws his liberty to do other things in order to accomplish the goal which he now desires. If one wants to build a family and have physical comforts in life, he has to restrict his freedom considerably in order to attain his goals. Nevertheless, he abandons his freedom and binds himself to a whole collection of obligations and responsibilities. Nothing worthwhile is accomplished in life without investing substantial time and energy, with the consequent loss of freedom to do other things. A business executive, a research chemist, a brain surgeon dedicate their whole lives to their objectives. But if the goal is justified, freedom may be sacrificed.

The Torah Jew also is dedicated to a goal that completely absorbs his life. The goal is to conquer death by conquering the forces in him that desire the physical and finite and by maximizing the forces in him that aspire to the spiritual and the eternal.

This split between the *neshama* (soul) and the body is a constant battle, raging every second of life. But the Torah uniquely explains how the Jew can reconcile this tension, using the physical to achieve the spiritual and devoting all his forces and abilities to a higher, sanctified purpose. The Torah Jew never denies physical need or pleasure. He says, however, that it is missing the point to use it only for its narrow physical enjoyment. Rather, the physical is a means to achieve the non-physical — the spiritual — in a way the Torah provides.

A classic example is drinking wine — certainly a pleasant physical experience. But the Torah Jew takes wine and sanctifies it, using it to make *kiddush* on Shabbat. Meaning: the wine is enjoyed not just for its taste and pleasant sensation but to celebrate and hallow the entrance of the spiritual dimension — Shabbat — into the weekly physical life of the Jew. The wine — used in moderation — demonstrates the blessings which Hashem has bestowed during the week. The delight as it lightens the heart tells the Jew that just as his body feels good, so too his *neshama* is on a higher plane on this special day of Shabbat. And it is precisely wine which is used, in order to indicate that just as wine has the potential to reduce man to his lowest physical state if used merely for personal pleasure, it also can help raise him to a sanctified state if used for spiritual pleasure. And so, too, all of life's physical aspects: if used as ends in themselves, they lower the Jew and can destroy him; but if used for the goal of serving the Creator, they can elevate him and make him more aware of his spiritual nature.

The Torah Jew, then, limits his freedom in order to actualize the most difficult goal on earth: transcending the physical to reach the spiritual. To fulfill this purpose, the Torah gives him a library full of learning, law, customs, restrictions, parables, examples. But compared to the individual who limits his freedom merely to accomplish physical ends, the Torah Jew becomes more free for every restriction which he obeys. How? Because these restrictions release him from his physical bonds and allow him to achieve a higher level of existence where the physical no longer governs. For example, instead of wine controlling his behavior, he controls wine, using it to perceive the spirituality of Shabbat. The person who uses wine only for its physical pleasure remains trapped in his bodily desires, trying to satisfy himself over and over again with the same passing joy that the wine brings. The satisfaction is temporary; yet he craves more, with the result that the wine makes him more of a slave to his appetites. The little bit of relief which he feels as the wine relaxes him is paid for heavily by its further conditioning him to yield to his physical impulses.

The Torah Jew, however, constrains himself under Torah guidelines so that he will cease being controlled by his animal nature and, gradually, gain an absolute freedom from it. He can then attain a deep and satisfying purity of action that brings true inner peace and joy. Instead of his nature dominating him, he dominates his nature. And this dominion is called meaningful choice and true freedom.

XV

INTIMATE LICENSE

We have touched upon the relatively neutral subject of wine as an illustration of the difference between the Torah and western culture in the approach to controlling human desires. The following brief discussion on the subject of male-female behavior patterns, however, is an even more fundamental example of the Torah-Jewish standard and, therefore, must be presented. Ordinarily, public discussion of such a topic would be highly discouraged because it could incite improper thoughts. But with Hashem's help, we shall attempt to compare the Torah-Jewish position on this most important of all issues.

Most people generally concede that a society stands or falls depending on the level of its sexual morality. From Sedom and Amora to the Roman Empire to the Third Reich, any culture is doomed if it perverts the most intimate of human relations.

Yet in western culture today, the standard has become so low that it is only a matter of time until there will be total collapse.

Under the label of individual freedom, the culture now tolerates an "anything goes" approach. Whatever the individual feels like doing is fine. The only test is whether he is having a good time and pursuing his desires without inhibitions. If he restrains himself, then he is "hung up" — artificially destroying his true nature. To give vent to his nature allows him license to put his fantasies into practice, and to indulge himself is a sign of his healthy adjustment to his animal instinct. Of course, he is not technically allowed to hurt anyone; so mutual consent becomes a pre-condition to full approval. But once this is present, he can live in his own so-called "paradise" without restraint.

This attitude in practice has resulted in promiscuity, human misery and the destruction of potential human beings. When the individual's desires set the standard, he starts wanting more and more, beginning his career early and never ceasing unless stopped; hunting in foreign pastures; legitimizing his animal cravings at the expense of his remaining morality; ignoring future consequences for the pleasure of the moment. In response to this ever-increasing looseness, the proliferation of birth-control methods has now "liberated" everyone where, before, only the professionally-knowledgeable few could behave so freely. This simple ticket to enjoyment is now a permit to act no differently from animals, for they, too, know no restraint. And along with this general degradation of human sensitivities, respect for life has been quietly abandoned, allowing the elimination of countless inconvenient unborn children. Somehow ignored is the ground rule that all is permissible so long as no one is hurt.

But the adults also do not escape unharmed. Animal behavior yields jungle results. No one is sure from day to day whether the hunt is on or not; who is hunting and who is being hunted; whether marital bonds matter or not; whether existing offspring are to be considered or not; whether yesterday's promises count today or not; whether emotions, sensitivities and mental well-being are important or not. And all these jungle-like uncertainties exist because the only criterion is whether the individual is having a good time at the present moment. He rules his heart of darkness and can decide without inhibitions. Therefore, whim and fancy become daily variables, unreliable and unstable as the weather and just as pervasive.

All this sordidness exists alongside western culture's fictional creation of romantic love. Romeo/ Juliet and Antony/Cleopatra are archetypes of the rose-colored glass through which the culture views the ideal male-female relationship. Falling in love with full moons, sparkling stars and string orchestras is the story-book plot which everyone is obliged to act out. Woe to the unfortunate one who loses the script or becomes tangled in the curtain ropes backstage! For he can no longer find "true happiness" or "live happily ever after." Indeed, he is doomed to an endless trek or wasteland of loneliness, vainly hoping for magic star-dust to fall on him, grabbing what partial companionship he can or alleviating his misery through lovelorn stories and songs.

The more sophisticated and thoughtful recognize that a couple's life together cannot be based merely on a physical-emotional attraction that depends on imagination and stage props and which can be changed at any time depending on the mood of the parties involved. So, to buttress their "love," these people rely on commitment, synergistic interaction and sincere, mutual responsibility. Yet, in truth, the basis of such "love" is still physical attraction, which, once satiated and exposed to the daily routine, is soon unglamorized and revealed as only a passing sensation.

Further, the system continues to depend on human preference and fancy. Tomorrow, one partner can change his decision because he remains always free to pursue his personal interest, which may no longer be compatible with his current relationship. Indeed, the more he bases his commitment on the honesty of his intentions, the more likely it is that life's variability will force him to admit honestly a change in his intentions. After all, to be true to himself is his first responsibility. His partner will "understand" because she also believes in honesty, emotional distress notwithstanding. Mutual com-

138

mitment, therefore, is equally unstable, being similarly subject to human partiality and weaknesses. Again we are left in the wilds, albeit more sophisticated, of human desires and inconstancy.

SANCTIFIED RELATIONS

One of the Torah Jew's most noted distinctions is that he strictly controls his interactions with the opposite sex. Indeed, we should continue our discussion under a following topic of marriage because only there does the Torah Jew consider the issue at all relevant.

A hallmark of the Jew over the centuries has been his fervent and stalwart opposition to any and all immorality and promiscuity. He abides by a strongly modest dress code. He never allows public mixed gatherings. He vehemently condemns all immodest displays of the human body. He completely prohibits premarital and extramarital relations. He does not permit his children from later childhood to young adulthood to associate with the opposite sex. There are no exhibitions of male-female closeness even in his home, much less on the street.

To understand why the Torah Jew behaves in

this fashion, one should avoid labels of "prudish" or "Victorian" and appreciate that just as the Torah Jew regulates his life under Torah guidelines in all other areas of human endeavor, he likewise follows Torah in matters of morality. The Torah desires that the Jew develop his capacity to sanctify himself. In no other single area of human behavior is the Torah more concerned that man preserve this potential than in the realm of intimate relations, which are the most prone to degenerate to an animal level. The sex drive can so dominate and captivate the human imagination and appetite that, unless it is properly controlled, the Jew can be pulled down by it and lose the potential to elevate it to its highest spiritual level. Everything physical in life was given by Hashem so that the Jew could raise it to its spiritual essence. Intimate relations are no different; in fact, they are the prime example how Torah edifies and magnifies the spiritual within the human being. This process is, obviously, not dependent on a human-reasoned set of rules. Rather, the Torah defines in this, as in all areas of life, specific details of proper conduct with the goal that the Torah Jew will — at the minimum — never abuse the human powers given him and — at the maximum — achieve an extraordinary level of human perfection and completeness.

So the Torah Jew is adamantly opposed to the slightest hint of moral degeneracy. What passes in western culture as living a freer, more uninhibited existence is to the Torah Jew no more than giving in to physical lust. Whatever rationalizations are made, whatever fancy words are expressed, whatever the level of sophisticated culture surrounding the issue, the basic truth is that, when people want to do something very much, many justifications can be found. And since intimate relations are highly desired, excuses are not lacking.

A favorite argument is that this desire is a natural physical urge and must be satisfied for the healthy operation of the human body. With this physical reality, the individual may with full approval do whatever he wants to satisfy himself. Though passing as logical, this approach is completely erroneous because it ignores the fundamental capacity and responsibility inherent in the Jew to raise the physical to the spiritual, to use material means to reach non-material ends. Thus, the Torah Jew never allows his physical instincts to operate only on that level. To do so would deny his purpose for being and reduce him to the level of an animal.

Instead, he uses his reproductive energies in a manner consistent with the spiritual guidelines of the Torah. The only way that he is ever allowed to use these powers is through the sanctity of marriage, because the Torah marriage is Hashem's approval that a couple may live together. Without His sanction, the individuals cannot live together. Further, within the marriage itself the Torah Jew obeys a whole section of rules on when and how these powers may be used (*taharat hamishpacha* — family purity). At all times he is on guard (in his thoughts as well as in his actions) that this most-difficult-to-restrain instinct stays under constant control. That which has brought countless cultures to ruin will never undo, with Hashem's help, the Torah Jew.

Today, many people would be amazed that a Torah Jew would not shake hands with a woman; that Torah women wear only dresses and never pants; that a Torah married woman completely covers her hair; that both explicit and implicit immodesty in newspapers, magazines, music, art, television and movies are absolutely forbidden. Surely what everyone takes for granted and thinks is harmless should be no cause for such severe concern and stringent rules. But the Torah Jew has not let his sensitivities be dulled by the promiscuous attitude of western culture. A norm that has accepted the public display of the human form in all varieties of personal and intimate relations must be rejected by the Torah Jew, who heralds the sanctity of human activity. To allow the human to appear and behave as a mere animal, thirsting for physical satisfaction, is an absolute degradation of man formed in the image of Hashem.

Further, what people think is harmless is no criterion, since their whole scale of sensitivities has become so lowered that what they find unobjectionable does not reach the level of acceptability on a higher scale. A Torah Jew so respects both the provocative power and the high sanctity of a woman (and vice versa) that he keeps distant from all women other than his wife, with whom he has become specially sanctified. Even if a situation would in most cases be devoid of overtones, familiarity in simple circumstances can lead to an attitude of closer familiarity in other cases. What starts innocently or casually may engender an easy outlook to women in general. The Torah Jew makes every effort to prevent his naturally susceptible senses from being stimulated in even the slightest degree, except within the sanctity of marriage. Moreover, the respect which he feels for the woman's unique life-giving role fortifies his resolve never to be involved in any situation that could lead him to forget, lessen or abuse her position. From here we see that Torah Judaism considers woman quite differently than western culture.

XVI

THE WESTERN-CULTURE WOMAN

We may say succinctly that western culture views
woman as the object of man's passion and the
keeper of his home. The recent movement of
women's "lib" has been a reaction to this view,
attempting to overturn the status of woman as
"object" and "house servant." Because western-culture man has looked on woman as a means to
satisfy his own pleasure and ignores her personal
needs, current discontent is endeavoring to change
the view of woman to give her more rights, respect
and independence.

So, today, a woman can behave with the same
free-style approach to her passions as a man does.
No more double standards. If she is viewed as an
object, then she has the right to view men as
objects. She can demand things exactly the way
that she wants them, and if they are not to her
liking, she can walk out. The same is true concern-

ing the home. Chains no longer bind her to household drudgery. Let the man scrub the floors, do the diapers — her career is just as important.

Even though this new model of woman is as yet applicable to only a small percentage of the population, since it is prevalent in the intellectual circles which Jews frequent it is a very live issue among Jewish women. And with their persistent effort, they may well succeed in making women exactly like men in everything but biological formation. Role parity and equal opportunity are the main rallying calls. Why should only the man go out into the competitive world? Why cannot women have the same responsibilities as men? Why does only the man get the opportunity to satisfy all his desires and quests? Although perfume sales are still higher among women, the goal of the new western-culture woman is to do all — or as many as possible — of the things that men do.

Preliminary indications are that while women are succeeding outwardly in their objective, distress rather than satisfaction has resulted inwardly. So now women take nerve pills and tranquilizers to cope with the competitive battle. Psychiatrists and psychologists now add women business executives to their appointment lists of businessmen. Salaries may be equal, but the money does not fulfill women's inner needs. And the more that they become successful like men, the less they find satisfaction on a personal level with men. A woman is no longer certain how to react. Should she show softness or should she hold firm? Is this a business deal or an emotional experience? On the man's side, even apart from envy and insecurity, he still would not prefer or feel comfortable with a woman who is striving to be like him. More of what he is used to on his side is not a particular appealing alternative.

Still, both sides make diligent attempts to cope, to compromise, to adapt, to please the other. The confusion of roles and expectations becomes so great that each day has the potential of bringing a new set of rules based on new individual desires. The tension and stress on the relationship are increased, and the longevity of the relationship is correspondingly decreased. The successful ones last because the partners finally resolve on some basic mode of living, which, according to this new model of woman, allows for separate vacations, alternate nights washing the dishes and separate checking accounts. Indeed, the ideal couple today is a perfect carbon copy — shirt, pants and hair style. If unisex has not yet arrived, it is certainly at the next to last stop.

A TORAH VIEW OF WOMAN

Observing the splendid economy of Hashem's creation, one could reasonably conclude that no part
duplicates another. Every component is an independent and distinct unit, interconnected but not
repetitive. Each element has a designated function
which it does best. The creation is perfect, and
every part of it is unique.

In addition, we find polarity and contrast: namely, up-down, right-left, lightness-darkness, positive-
negative, protons-electrons, force-counterforce, ac-
tive-passive, centrifugal-centripetal. The interplay
of these combinations sets in motion the whole of
the natural world's movement and creativity. Despite the over-simplicity of this model, one still sees
the mutual exclusivity of the polarities. There is
interaction but not intermingling. The parts perform as a unit, but each is a separate entity. Neither
is a duplicate of the other, and each has its own

special role, which cannot be altered to become like its partner.

So the Torah Jew has a very clear picture of the roles of the man and of the woman: one cannot fully function without the other, but each has a separate task to fulfill. The Creator who set the planets in orbit and ordered the workings of a beehive also established the proper areas of activity of man and woman. He who created human beings knows best how they should optimally function. And the Torah explains for the Jew what that best way is.

The Torah man and woman are both dedicated to creating the world of the spirit in the physical realm, returning the presence of the Creator to His creation. The effort to accomplish this goal requires a partnership, each taking on different prime responsibilities. Just as in any partnership, each partner uses his particular talents to maximize the success of the enterprise.

Each Jew is considered half a person until he marries. Then he finds his complement, namely, that part of his potential whole being that was lacking. Clearly the addition must be different from what already existed. It is no carbon copy, because instead of completing the new entity, it would merely repeat the original half. Indeed, biology establishes that the only procreative unit is a non-duplicative one. Also in metallurgy, for example, the combination of distinct and unique elements forms an alloy different from its components. To create the new whole of a Torah-Jewish couple, each side contributes a dynamic entity that complements the other so that what was two parts is now one unified whole.

One aspect of the Torah Jew's having been formed in the image of Hashem is his capacity to create. Just as Hashem created all of existence, so too the Torah Jew in his small realm has a part in creating.

The division of this ability between male and female is the basic indicator of the distinct roles each brings to the marriage. The Torah woman primarily creates physically; the Torah man primarily creates spiritually. In their building a Torah home together, they create harmony, completeness, peace, each using his full energies to maximize his particular specialty.

The Torah man learns Torah during as many hours of the day as possible. The Torah has the potential to transform all physical reality into pure, spiritual reality. The creation of this special dimension is primarly the occupation of the Torah male. It takes endless hours of immensely arduous toil to comprehend the thoughts of Hashem in His Torah and to internalize this learning into his personality and behavior. To strive to make himself more in the image of Hashem is the only true creation that a Jew can personally accomplish during his time on earth.

The Torah woman is the complement of the man. The two together form the best and only combination for attaining their mutual and individual fulfillment. Her prime responsibility is creation in the physical realm, and in this area she feels the greatest satisfaction. The woman's desire to bear children despite all the difficulties and pain reflects her need to create in the way that she can best do so.

But her creation does not end just with nurturing the fetus and giving birth. A birth without continued nurturing is an incomplete creation. The Torah woman creates a home, an atmosphere, an environment where not only do her children receive their foundation of life but also her husband receives the haven and support without which he could not create in his prime area of activity. And the Torah woman understands that her role is the necessary complement of her husband's; that each part is equal, separate and dependent on the other; that each in his way contributes to a unit which can succeed only if each concentrates on his special function.

Most people realize that a child's early years set the pattern for his entire life. The Torah woman builds for her children a firm basis of love, giving, concern, self-confidence, which establishes a positive and creative base for the Jewish child's entire subsequent development. That the woman is primarily involved in this beginning is because, generally, her psychological composition tends to emotional warmth, supportive caring and selfless giving — all in greater intensity than in the male. The biological connection — pregnancy, birth and nursing

— is a physical indicator of a deeper psychological relationship that binds mother with child in the all-important beginning stage of the child's preparation for life. The mother's close attention and concern are the essential emotional building blocks with which the child can successfully surmount life's initial challenges. Feeling the security of his mother's love and care, the child can mature step by step to full independent behavior.

The Torah woman's success, however, does not depend solely on her loving care and peaceful home. What is all crucial is her commitment to Hashem and His Torah. Upon her dedication to follow the will of Hashem the children are able to build all their subsequent growth in becoming full Torah Jews. She is the first to teach the children how to say the *berachot* (blessings); she makes certain that they are ready and eager when the *cheder* (school) bus comes in the morning; she is the one who packs the little cookie bags when they go to shul with father on Shabbat evening. It is the mother who sows the seed of love for Torah. And her pure devotion may be a reason why she receives equal reward for all the Torah learning of her children.

For a different reason, this reward is also earned for her husband's learning. Because of her self-sacrifice in taking on as much of the physical burdens as possible — including part-time employment, plus a measure of loneliness when her husband is away learning — she shares equally in the spiritual rewards of her husband's Torah learning. Today we call this division of functions specialization. But in Torah terms, the woman is simply doing the role outlined for her by Hashem,* which includes a hundred other deeds of lovingkindness in assisting the aged, the orphaned, the widowed, the poor, those as yet unmarried. The Torah family succeeds when each partner contributes his particular function, creating a whole entity serving Hashem.

The advocates of exchanging roles have, perhaps, not studied well the early history of the Jewish People. When Pharoah and the Egyptians were looking for ways to oppress their Jewish slaves, they choose a particularly cruel measure. They switched the roles of men and women: the men worked in the house; the women, in the fields. In revealing this incident, the Torah is not discussing role-conditioning or even the physical and emotional limitations of the different sexes. The lesson may be more fundamental. The Creator obviously created everything for a purpose and that purpose was set from the beginning. The Torah explains and defines the purpose and function of everyone and everything. When one goes against this system, he is trying to undo the creation, bringing havoc and misery to all concerned. What is often lacking on the part of these advocates of change is an inside knowledge

* As explained by Rav Baruch Horovitz, the Torah describes an ascending degree in the creation of earthly creatures, with woman created last. Therefore, she is a more whole and perfect being and does not require that degree or type of correction which man needs.

of and living experience with the Torah life-style. The Jew without Torah in western culture is unfortunately misled in many areas, and altering Jewish male-female roles is no exception.

XVII

MARRIAGE

The concept of marriage is currently changing so frequently that any description will probably be overtaken by time. Still, there seems to be a general direction, useful as a working definition. Whereas marriage was once viewed as a social convention of more or less permanence, lately it is considerably less permanent and, for some, no longer even a social convention.

We see that people marry because it is the thing to do — with reasons sometimes, and sometimes even without reasons. The ceremony has become so devoid of real meaning that those who enjoy ignoring social amenities simply skip the formalities. And those who are less non-conforming satisfy their gnawing uncertainty by saying, "Well, if it doesn't work out, we can always get a divorce."

Very often, the main reason for marrying is that it is the only next step. Societal expectation, public appearances, legality on the record books — all influence the decision to marry. Having a religious wedding is a side matter of taste or parental pressure; registration at city hall is the main thing. Indeed, the legal formalities somehow tarnish the romanticism that imagines undisturbed lovebirds residing in their nest. Yet, marriage is an institution, and as the joke goes, who wants to be in an institution? So even when people succumb, they do not really know what has happened, apart from "Mr. & Mrs." on the front door and on charge-account cards. When they further consider that this new apparatus can with ease be disassembled, their sense of insecurity at the whole process intensifies.

Of course, some prefer to have a man in religious garb utter incantations and aphorisms over the special event. It gives more meaning and helps make a lovely wedding, but what that meaning is exactly is not explained or understood. The parties have made a public resolution to attempt to live together and form a family. But why, for what purpose, under whose auspices — are left unanswered.

As noted, these formalities and customs are increasingly being ignored because people see little real meaning or content in them. Since marriage has become expendable, people now establish "honest" relationships, which last as long as mutually convenient. Legalities, after all, are annoying and unnecessary impositions on simple, natural human behavior. So why bother?

All these approaches have created even greater instability and confusion in the prime societal structure — the family. Those who marry without real purpose soon find that romanticism is not enough to keep them together. It is good for the movies and novels, but it passes like a cloud. Further, whereas once social convention maintained them as a couple after the "honeymoon," today the trend has turned in the opposite direction. Being divorced is just as acceptable as being married. In fact, the ever-increasing divorce propensity will soon make a second divorce the popular norm. And since marriage is so little understood, how can it protect itself from being further undermined?

Once the foundation stone of society crumbles, everything else falls. Even the most normal children are put off-balance. They are often deprived in some measure of their basic emotional needs of stability and affection, sometimes below the critical point. Identity confusion, split loyalties, distrust, insecurity, a sense of loss — all are potential maladjustments. No doubt the definition of "normal" will change, but clearly the standard has been lowered. And how will these children approach setting up a family unit for their own children? (Indeed, this problem has already affected the current generation.)

Some say that marriage and the family are no longer needed. But inherent, organic societal systems can no more easily be eliminated than limbs of the body. Besides the trauma to children, adults

themselves suffer tremendously from the free attitude to marriage. Loneliness and deep sadness per-
vade. Endless searching and vain attempts prevail.
Parents without partners are torn and tossed. Loose
morals and callousness proliferate; having lost a
fixed standard, people behave as if no standard
exists. They try to cope and manage, but the ignorance which they started with just keeps growing.
And the carousal at the wedding feast is replaced
by a depressing and pointless merry-go-round.

TORAH MARRIAGE

Consistent with the whole tenor of the Torah life-style, the Torah Jew's approach to marriage is not "Am I getting what I want?" but "What does Hashem want me to do?" Building a family is one of Hashem's mitzvot and is to be performed just like all the other mitzvot. Contemporary fads and view-points, obviously, do not alter the eternal mitzvot, and the family is still and always will be the basic Torah social unit.

Marriage is a deliberate action, planned and designed to fulfill a specific function. Romance, physical attraction and societal expectation are not the critical motivations for marriage. The decision to marry comes about because the Torah Jew wants to perform the will of the Creator. Hashem's will is that people procreate and that they sanctify their power to procreate through marriage. As dis-cussed, the Torah constantly directs the Jew to take the physical and elevate it to the spiritual. The sexual drive is a prime example of the use of the physical to serve the Creator. Not for personal pleasure do Torah Jews marry but in order to raise a family of Torah children who will follow Hashem's will, continuing their forefathers' heritage and becoming a light unto the nations.

So, with a modesty and self-restraint unknown to western culture, a young man in his early 20's and a young woman around 20 form a sanctified family unit, pure and completely unsullied by the undertones of western attitudes. Far more mature than their untutored-in-Torah contemporaries, they have been guided by their parents in making their decision, secure in several overriding principles:

— Hashem has specially arranged that they should meet;
— their match was ordained from the beginning of time;
— their marriage is for a lifetime;
— the purpose of their marriage is to fulfill Hashem's Torah.

As mentioned, each Jew is considered only half a person until he marries. Then the parts become whole and can complete their mission in creation. The Torah Jew realizes that marriage is an essential element in his ability to serve Hashem with a complete *neshama* and body. Only then is he able to use all his powers for the purpose for which they were created, under rules and an ethos which further spiritualize his existence. For example, many have heard of the Jewish family purity laws (*taharat hamishpacha*), which have become renowned because of their salutary effects. But two of their primary purposes are to engender sexual control and to develop increased consideration for one's partner.

The Torah-Jewish family has been and continues to be the framework through which the Jewish nation fulfills its Torah mission. It can accomplish this purpose precisely because it avoids the world of primarily egocentric love-fascination and mutual-convenience pacts, where the center of the family unit is the inconstant human being. Instead of the tragic road of meaninglessness, promiscuity and divorce, the Torah home goes in exactly the opposite direction through a definite pattern of joy and discipline. Torah and mitzvot infuse the Jewish home: the weekly Shabbat, the festivals, the special occasions of *brit milah*, *pid'yon haben*, bar mitzva and weddings, the teaching of the children, the husband-wife Torah relationship. This dynamic and positive system creates a home of love and purpose wherein the Jew can actualize his spiritual potential in the full service of Hashem. His marriage is no social convention or haphazard human experiment. On the contrary, by following the Torah, he is building a home in which Hashem's presence can dwell.

161

XVIII

WEDDINGS

Everybody loves a wedding. There are smiles and laughter, joyful tears and gladsome conviviality. The young man and woman who were only "yesterday" a boy and girl have grown up to become a husband and wife. Just amazing.

But what is the purpose of the wedding? In western culture, a wedding is a ceremonial feast. Except for the civil legalities, which can also be done by a municipal employee, the occasion is a good excuse to make merry, become intoxicated and let loose. A cleric's few pious statements add a certain seriousness. But real quick, let's have an hors d'oeuvre and a drink.

And what a display of food and drink is brought forth! The lushness of the affair is amply proved by the huge quantities thrown away at the evening's end, including roses, carnations, petits fours, ice swans, candles, wedding souvenirs, and the special poem or song in honor of the newly-weds. How something so short-lived could cost so much is a good question. Never mind, the important thing is whether the wedding was more glamorous than others, whether the dresses were beautiful, whether the guests enjoyed the food, whether the orchestra played well, whether the festivities ended late enough. And, of course, the memorial picture album, which preserves the evanescent grandeur for countless living-room guests.

For the bride and groom, the event is so rushed and superficial that they are barely aware of what is happening. It is not enough that they are the center of attraction. They must also be host and hostess for the whole assemblage. Congratulating cousin Harry on his promotion may be pleasant conversation, but the reception line still has a long way to go, not to mention visiting all the tables. It is no wonder that they have to escape from everyone and leave parents, family and friends for a "honeymoon."

THE TORAH WEDDING

Both marriage and the technical process of becoming married are mitzvot of Hashem. So the tone of a Torah Jewish wedding is entirely different from the good time of a western-culture wedding. One has a pleasant experience, certainly. But that is not the purpose of the wedding.

The whole proceeding is for the sanctification and spiritual elevation of the *chatan* (groom) and *kalla* (bride). This day is like a Yom Kippur for them; they fast and work on themselves to be cleansed of all past wrong-doings, and Hashem re-creates them as new beings. All who watch this happening feel a spiritual and joyous "high." They enjoy the lovely decorations, the festive food and joyous dancing (men and women separately). But what makes them happy is knowing that two more Jews have been granted a new and higher stage of serving Hashem. And such a happiness is worth

dancing about in order that the *chatan* and *kalla*
— so serious in their individual preparations — will
share in the joy that all the People Israel feels
when two of its members have received their eternal
partners.

And the *chatan* and *kalla* have only to sit back
and be entertained and honored. They are king and
queen and must not even fatigue themselves by
dancing overmuch. If they want a glass of water,
someone brings it for them. Everyone at the wedding has only one desire: to increase the happiness
of the *chatan* and *kalla*. This one does acrobatics,
that one a pantomime; the next dances balancing
a tray of bottles on his chin, and still another does
comedy antics. The consumption of alcoholic bever-
ages is negligible, yet everyone dances and sings
with such fervor and excitement that it is clear that
they are "high" — uplifted and extremely overjoyed
doing the mitzva of making the *chatan* and *kalla*
happy. No one has come just to have a good time
for himself. Rather, he is there to help others enjoy
themselves. Of course, the more one gives, the more
one receives in return. The greatest happiness comes
when, in giving himself over fully to causing joy,
the individual and his ego become absorbed in the
elation of the whole. The stronger he dances in
order to lift even higher the spirit of the *chatan*
and *kalla*, the more he himself becomes uplifted
and transcends all limitations of time and space.

One sees in this example of Hashem's mitzvot
how they work to release the individual from his

egocentricity by encouraging and prompting him to give to others. The more he gives, the more he removes his limitations. The more mitzvot he constantly does, the more he makes himself like the One Who is continuously giving him life. And, in the meantime, look at all the joy that can be created! Nothing compares to a Torah-Jewish wedding for clean, inspiring happiness where vibrant human energy is completely directed to selfless goals.

XIX

THE SYNAGOGUE

Well-known is the degree to which the synagogue has become an infrequent habitation, except on special occasions: the High Holidays, bar mitzvas and weddings. Historically the center of Jewish life, it has become supplanted today by the country club, the health spa and the shopping center. Rivaling its competitors, the synagogue offers a wide variety of social attractions in an effort to hold its membership: men's clubs, sisterhoods, evening socials, bazaars, lectures, concerts.

And consistent with the general rule (the more one is empty on the inside, the more he dresses up on the outside), the synagogue has become an architectural palace, bedecked with draperies and matching carpets, highlighted by recessed illumination and modern art. Huge halls with spiring ceilings are tributes to the mounting economic resources of the Jewish population. But a hollow echo rings in these auditoriums, empty nine-tenths of the time. Most of the week-day praying takes place in a small side room, reminding one of the fallen fortunes of a theater star now consigned to the back stage. Indeed, the whole production on the front stage seems very distant and artificial, like a show with an audience watching, or with occasional audience participation, as on morning television programs.

The innovative efforts of "rabbis" to make "services-in-the-round" and "rap" sessions are apt testimony to an otherwise dull and meaningless experience. Not that there is not enough talk and interest in other things: clothes, sports, business... And with the mixing together of men and women, the whole purpose of the synagogue is smothered in the fashion show, fine perfumery and diverted attentions.

But the mainstay of the synagogue today is its education of children. Young Jewish couples first consider synagogue affiliation when they realize that their growing child should know something about Judaism. Nothing that the child learns, however, should disturb the limited knowledge which the parents have, nor should the education cause any changes in their lives. It is sufficient if the parents think that they are fulfilling their sense of obligation to educate their children Jewishly.

The synagogue does attempt to teach adults — under the same proviso as the children: "No changes in your life! " From his well-designed pulpit, the "rabbi" impresses his congregation with his erudition and elocution. His continued success depends on his capacity to appear to say something but actually say nothing. Then, no one is offended and everyone is satisfied. Likewise, the adult education classes resemble informal college evening courses, with much discussion — and no conclusions that make any difference in the participants' lives.

All the efforts to make the synagogue service and activities "relevant," meaningful and engaging have yielded no lasting results; the people simply are not interested. Some serious-minded individuals, however, have formed their own Jewish collectives where they directly attempt a personal spiritual experience through poetry, meditation, singing, dancing, social-political action and — increasingly — learning the actual Torah sources. These independent, iconoclastic Jews could not possibly accept the Judaism which they see in the synagogue. What they are searching for is truth, the truth of Torah. As they continue on their path, eventually they will come to a full acceptance of Torah and mitzvot which will allow them to tap the full depth of their Jewish awareness and energies — perhaps very soon.

THE TORAH SYNAGOGUE

Many people are fond of calling their office their second home. Some spend more time there than at their house. For the Torah Jew, the synagogue — the *Beit K'nesset/Beit Midrash* — is his second home and, in some cases, first. What makes this place so dear to him?

He knows the language being used (Hebrew), and he knows what is going on. The *davening* (prayers) is as much a part of him as his own name. Indeed, along with the other men, he takes turns leading the services, for there are no performers and no audience here; everyone is an active participant in every part of the proceedings.

The Torah synagogue (*shul*) is a very special place because here the Jew finds tranquility and communication with Hashem. Therefore, the surroundings are modest though tidy, with nothing to distract his deep concentration. The room is large enough, but not overbearing. The furnishings are practical and simple: tables, straight wooden chairs and benches, bookcases, plain curtains. The one object that is enhanced is the ark with its cover. Since the scroll of the Torah is inside, it receives the most honored and adorned treatment. The serious activity at hand is uninterrupted by side conversations, idle activity or going in and out. So-called "sermons" are almost non-existent. The dress is practically indistinguishable since each married man wears a *tallit* (prayer shawl) which covers the majority of the body.

Consistent with the Torah sensitivities mentioned in Chapter XV, the women daven in a separate section. More than likely, the Torah woman prefers davening at home — her realm of influence — since her basic nature is to be inside, within, modest, out of the public gaze. Because intellectually, emotionally and physically, she completes herself through internal activities, she leaves the public functions to the men, who have just the opposite role of external activity.

The mood of the Torah synagogue reflects an awareness that prayer is one of the world's pillars. Simplicity, humility and deep concentration permeate the atmosphere. Since each makes the shul a regular part of his day — indeed, three times per day — the rhythm and pace of the davening become ingrained in the mind and heart. The chain of tradition extends for several millennia, but each Jew is required to contemplate his words carefully and to add personal petitions from his heart in order to ensure a spontaneity that will bring him closer to the Creator. Being graded in school and on the job is not so very different from being tested by Hashem, the only distinction being that Hashem tests everything, all the time! So the Jew learns to test himself and considers his thoughts and words very attentively when he specially presents his case before Hashem. The Father who hears everything and sustains everyone will answer truly sincere and humble requests. The Jew just has to crack a small, honest opening in his busy importance and supposed independence. His efforts, when joined with at least nine other Jewish males (a *minyan*), acquire a special dynamic power as a whole which is greater than the sum of its parts. Since the *minyan* represents the Jewish People, it can help complete the mission of the Jewish People by joining individual resources in a united effort to make Hashem's sovereignty more manifest in the world. Upon occasion, without public knowledge, the roofs of some shuls have even been suspected of lifting up just a little bit through the intensity of the davening being directed from below.

But the real distinction of the Torah shul is that Jews learn Torah there. Whereas prayer is the Jew communicating with Hashem, learning Torah is Hashem communicating with the Jew. Indeed, for every measure of any other shul activity, there is a double and triple measure of learning. The whole foundation of the Jew is his learning of Torah; so, naturally, the shul — the center of Jewish communal existence — is the place where he uses his time to learn. Sometimes he learns alone or with a friend; at other times, a rav gives a *shiur* (class) where a common text is studied, questions are asked and a lively discussion ensues. The age of this Torah Jew who makes such full use of his shul is anywhere from seven to a hundred and seven. In other words, the shul is the fertile soil of the Jew's growth: a place where he can nurture his potential of understanding and becoming like Hashem — to the degree that a mortal human is capable. That this process is real, active, fulfilling and passionately lived can be seen by visiting Torah shuls and observing Jews of all ages, from those with flowing white beards to those still red in the cheeks, learning Chumash, Mishna, Gemara, *Tehillim* (Psalms), halacha, mussar and chassidut.

Many impressive synagogues today richly decorate the ark and pulpit platform with a *ner tamid* (eternal light). This light is a remembrance of the Gold Menorah that once was in the *Beit Hamikdash* (the Holy Temple) and whose central olive-oil-drawing wick was never extinguished. One can understand from the Torah shul, however, what that light was intended to represent: the light of perfect wisdom and behavior that comes from studying the Torah of Hashem. The décor of a Torah shul may be less elegant, but the light therein is infinitely more brilliant.

XX

THE WESTERN-CULTURE THIRST

Mentioned before was western culture's thirst for physical consumption. Whatever is bigger, fancier, richer is better. The culture fosters the instinct of the ego to show its supremacy through its physical accomplishments. Everyone tries to show his best, the show on the outside proving that he is successful, important, worthwhile. Thus, conspicuous consumption of clothes, cars, homes, jewelry and vacations not only keeps the economy going but also sustains people in their self-image.

Such a measure of success, however, is quite expensive and may take the efforts of not only most of the day but also most of a life to achieve. Moreover, every addition to the structure becomes an integral part of the ego, indispensably feeding the constant need for approval and self-confidence. Soon, a whole edifice of luxuries become necessities, and a person can make of himself a castle, walled in by all the blocks of his physical empire.

Even those who content themselves with a small chateau, once having created their self-image on the basis of these achievements, are loathe to alter the structure. They and their physical environment have become inseparable. (Now we see why, as people get older, they become more conservative — because they are consistently defining themselves through their possessions. On the other hand, youth remains open and exploring because, not having as yet amassed many possessions, it has not fixed its identity). The more possessions one has, the more one has defined and is content with his self-image because each reinforces the other. In the end, a person and his things become identical. He *is* the house in the country; he *is* the man with a fancy car; he *is* the natty dresser.

Such a way of life makes it very difficult for people to separate themselves from their physical possessions. No wonder the ancient Pharoahs loaded their tombs with their wealth! Though today people realize that "you can't take it with you," they hold on to it dearly until the bitter end. Then the next generation also tries, only again to lose hold at the end. But the cycle continually repeats itself, as each bases his self-image on his possessions.

THE WATERS OF TORAH

The person on the outside looking in may object that the Torah life-style appears impractical. If the Jew is learning Torah all day, how does he put bread and butter on the table? The answers lie in the Torah attitude to physical possessions, which is entirely different from that of western culture.

The Jew's self-image does not depend on his physical possessions. His identity is defined by his ascending capacity to come closer to the knowledge of Hashem. This effort to achieve the non-physical is channeled through the physical—his mental capacity to learn Torah and his corporeal energy to do mitzvot. Though ultimately his Torah activity will be motivated without thought of personal gain, Torah does act as a means to move the Jew away from an external definition of self—physical possessions—to an internal definition of self—the perfection and refinement of character and personality. That which is within him is the non-physical; that which is outside him is the physical, and the Torah Jew concentrates on the former.

In other words, he does not want to have, to possess; he wants to be, to become, to make himself better.* The whole process of Torah is to take his poorer characteristics and improve them. So, for example, if he is prone to anger, by learning Torah he internalizes a living awareness that Hashem is causing *everything* in the whole universe to exist, and, therefore, he need not be angry if a certain thing does not go his way. Hashem obviously knows better than he how the world should be run. Whereas this description may seem simple, anyone who has been angry knows that controlling temper is very difficult at the pressure point. But this kind of test and the Torah's ability to help the Jew to meet it are what make life worthwhile and truly challenging.

The Jew's effort to reform himself in the name of Hashem and His Torah reveals to all mankind the true greatness of the Creator: first, that He is Magnificent in creating the physical world *and* providing the means to perfect it; and, second, that He is so Humble as to give mortal man an opportunity to exist with Him when, in reality, He has no need for him at all. In response to these aspects of Hashem's greatness, Torah Jews accept the obligation to emulate Him and follow His Torah in

* See Rav Aryeh Carmell, *Strive for Truth*, "On Good Ambitions," p. 140, Feldheim Publishers Ltd., Jerusalem, 1978.

order that His "effort" in creating man will not have been in vain.

It is in vain when the Jew goes about his business ignoring Hashem and not doing the task which He gave him to do — "Perfect yourself according to the way which I told you." By making life a matter of *having*, possessing, buying, consuming, a person misses the purpose of his existence: *to become*, to be a totally better human being. To the degree that he occupies himself with "having" and ignores "becoming," the individual resembles the depositor of money in a bank that is bound to fail. His physical currency ends when he physically ends. But a person who puts his deposits into "becoming" (i.e., working on his non-physical aspects) credits his account in a bank that exists forever. He earns shares for eternity because every improvement in character completes the ultimate purpose of creation and, thereby, allows Hashem to reward him beyond the confines of physical birth and death. The best estate planning allows the testator to be the beneficiary! And the Torah Jew realizes that the all-powerful and all-kind Creator intended life only for his benefit — for now and forever — if only he shows an interest and acceptance of the way that He explained how that life should be used.

Therefore, it is not hard to imagine why the Torah Jew rarely has steak on his table, or three-layer chocolate cakes, or a two-car garage, or a vacation in Florida. His income effort is minimal, just enough to provide the physical necessities, plus money with which to do the mitzvot. The huge majority of his time — as much as he possibly can afford — is used to learn Torah and do mitzvot. These two main activities enable him to *become* more perfect. The striving to possess yields no permanent remuneration. So, it is clearly better to forego the alluring physical abundance, content oneself with enough to live on, and put one's efforts into that which endures forever: adherence to the will of Hashem. The waters of Torah quench the real thirst for meaningful living.

XXI

WESTERN-CULTURE QUESTS

Of course, not everyone is striving only for physical possessions. In fact, most thinking people would be dissatisfied with their lives if they did not attach some higher purpose or goal to their existence. Some hope that they can make the world a somewhat better place as a result of their having been alive. Others strive to make a major breakthrough in their field of endeavor or profession, some theory, analysis, research, practical application that has never existed before. And still others extend their goals to a full-ranged reform program: nuclear disarmament, peace in the Middle East, defending the rights of the poor and disadvantaged, battling corruption, crime and corporations, striking out at hypocrisy, provincialism... Indeed, just being kind to other people is an admirable goal.

In addition, many Jewish people, who sense a dimension above the physical, experiment with other searches for truth and meaning: transcendental meditation, drugs, mystical cults, foreign religions, sensitivity groups, poetry, nature hikes. In fashion or out of fashion, alone or in groups, short-term or on-going — "you name it and they've tried it! "

None of these answers is completely satisfying because they do not involve the totality of the Jew's activities. For example, a person gets a "high" from one of these experiences, but then has to come "down" to normal activity. Sometimes there may be a residual effect, but generally his life is split between these highs and lows. Moreover, after a while, every experiment "burns out." The once attractive path to truth is no longer fruitful or complete, and now something else has to be tried. One new "trip" after another, one new cause after another until, finally, the experimenter settles down into some comfortable life pattern that he admits is not all that he wants, resigning himself either to his own limitations or to the limitations inherent in life.

THE TORAH SEARCH

For both the Jew who wants to achieve a higher reality and the Jew who simply wants to improve the quality of his life, Torah offers a complete program guaranteed to produce results. Why does Torah succeed where everything else fails?

Apart from it being the clear dictate of Hashem and apart from its successful implementation by Jews for the past 3300 years, Torah succeeds because it forces the individual to face the truth every moment of the day.

In a world that accepts no or little truth, people accustom themselves to non-truth-oriented life-styles, flowing along with the crowd and accepting the current expediency. But the people who are searching realize innately that there is a truth. Unfortunately, though, they are being misled or bogged down in systems that are partial or non-truths, but not the whole truth. Torah is the whole truth.

185

For example, people often convince themselves that they are very bright and intelligent. Torah forces them to see that they are not as smart as they think they are — obviously, a very important truth to learn! How? Through learning Gemara, which constantly challenges the brain beyond its point of comprehension. The Torah also sharpens the intellect to a higher level of comprehension, but, at the same time, a point of unintelligibility is reached where again the individual learns humility.

People often think that they are beautiful and charming. The Torah forces them to see the truth: whatever qualities one possesses are gifts to be used under certain conditions. For example, it is a mitzva for a married Jewish woman to cover her hair. She shows respect for her power of attraction by using her beauty in the way that Hashem directs her. If the individual uses his gifts just for himself, they become spoiled and corrupting. But if they are turned to the service of their Giver, then they blossom and shine with true beauty. The pure radiance of Torah-Jewish women forces a person to lower his eyes.

People expend their prime efforts to acquire material possessions. Torah teaches such an individual that he is pursuing vanity and wasting his time. He goes to dust and his money goes to his children. The many lessons of our forefathers prove that what lasts for all time is not the inheritance of money. For, indeed, how many generations back can a physical legacy be traced? Whereas the Jewish spiritual inheritance goes back 3300 years, untainted and undevaluated by time. When the Jew learns the *real* Jewish history and lives in an environment that embodies the moral and spiritual lessons of that history, he cannot fool himself that if he makes more net income this year, he is better off than last year.

People like to believe that they are honest and good. It may well be that they are to some degree, but the ingrained bias factor can considerably inflate the reality. Torah relentlessly forces a person to face the truth about himself. A Jew is required to learn halacha — the basic rules by which he is to lead his life. One rule requires a man of means to give money to the poor until their needs be satisfied. Now, he may convince himself that he is being "good" when he gives 2% of his income to *tzedaka* (the rightful due of the needy). But it turns out that the bare minimum is 10%, and if he wants to show that he really cares, he can give up to 20%. And if he is considerably well-to-do, being "good" can cost him a lot more. When it is in his interest, a person's conscience can be satisfied by a lower performance level of "good" than what actually is good. Torah gives him the constant opportunity to test his self-estimation against a true standard of good. Then he cannot continually fool himself within his self-contained world of biased and rationalized "truth."

Even where his view of truth on one issue happens to coincide with Torah truth, when he learns

Torah he will soon find that his views in countless other areas do not correspond to actual truth. Torah has a built-in system that trains him to stick to the truth and not to vacillate or fudge the situation to suit his momentary need. The Torah Jew learns that he is living in a world that is continuously under the supervision of Hashem; nothing happens without Hashem's personal direction. Hashem knows the Jew's every thought and deed. Gradually developing this level of awareness through Torah learning and mitzvot, he realizes that if he deviates from the truth in even the slightest degree, he will gain nothing but trouble. Also, because his appreciation of Hashem's ever-presence is increasing, he will want naturally to do the right thing in order to maintain and further his good relations with the Creator.

Many more examples could be given of the truth-searching potential in Torah. It is so powerful and dynamic that it can revolutionize the world. Unfortunately, as in the famous parable of the poor tailor and his dream of the pot of gold under the distant bridge, there is a tendency to search elsewhere rather than in one's back yard for what is most precious. If the Jew will seriously and intensively look into his own Torah heritage, he will discover all he needs and far more.

XXII

THE WORLD RELIGIONS

Already mentioned is the pluralism that ascribes equality of truth to all thought systems and religions. As a very small minority among systems that loom like goliaths over him, the Jew who does not know about Torah can very likely suffer a latent but huge inferiority complex. After all, "How can I be right and they all be wrong!" And since the Torah explains that no lie can stand without some truth in it, the unknowing Jew in a non-Jewish environment is in a very uncomfortable position:

(1) Either he can believe that truth is in many different places, a principle that does not really help him to know what he particularly is supposed to do or feel pride in;

(2) or he can believe that truth, being everywhere, is in no particular place and, therefore, since everyone cannot be right, he will avoid in-

volvement in the whole affair;

(3) or he can continue on a "Jewish-style" path that gives very little real meaning to his life, but at least allows him to allay his conscience, which tells him that being Jewish is important and worthwhile even if he does not know exactly why;

(4) or he can abandon the pretense of his "minority" Judaism and join the band-wagon majority.

All these unfortunate alternatives exist only because of one fact: ignorance. If the Jew knew what Torah Judaism is, he would laugh at the absurdity of adopting any of these options.

But first, let us examine more closely the attitude to the various religions.

Suffering enough through the ages from the "loving" approach that other religions have to the Jew, the Jew naturally advocates, at the very least, peaceful coexistence. "Leave me alone, and I won't bother you either." The Jew in this situation will do nothing that makes him stick out as a Jew. He may change his Jewish-sounding name. He will not object to working on Shabbat or the Jewish holidays. He will be very sensitive to suspicions of dual loyalty to countries where other Jews live. Of course, he attends the office "winter" party and mails "season's-greetings" cards. He will pattern his life-style almost exactly like any non-Jew, from afternoon cocktail to favorite sports team, to washing the car on Sundays, to reading the latest best seller.

At the same time, he is allowed a certain amount of Jewish identity. On Rosh Hashanah and Yom Kippur he is expected to take off from work. He can be known as a connoisseur of kosher salami and Jewish rye bread. When a sports or movie star is Jewish, he feels a share in some of the fame. When Israel manages to survive another Arab attempt to destroy it, he can feel pride that Jews are not always so easily butchered.

Even so, this defensive position leaves him wide-open to attack. His children want to have a "decorated tree" in the house just like the neighbors. His son wants to date this non-Jewish girl who also likes bagels and lox very much. His promotion is considered very scrupulously to see if there is *anything* unfavorable. And as a final shock, after centuries of anti-Jewish oppression against Jews up until this very day, he is completely bewildered to find that his searching and sensitive daughter has joined the opposition, having been convinced that her Judaism and a so-called religion of "love" are completely compatible.

The position of the young and aware Jew with almost no background in Torah Judaism is particularly beleaguered. He can find no reasonable rebuttal to what the non-Jewish majority persuasively presents to him. He already believes that there is no difference between him and a non-Jew. For a long time now, he has rejected meaningless rituals and consistently fought hypocritical behavior. Further, he truly wants peace, brotherhood and the unity of all mankind. Removing all barriers, making everyone the same, communicating on a basic emotional level — these are the "true" answers to the world's problems. And the first step is to agree with what the non-Jews say is good for the Jews. After all, perhaps the Jews have not been tolerant enough, giving enough, loving enough.

THE UNIQUE JEW

One of the most frightening and, at the same time, most exciting experiences is for the individual to discover that he is different from everyone else. The function of life and education is to develop the uniqueness of each person and have him actualize his particular capacities for both his fullest benefit and the joint benefit of the whole.

If anyone fails to receive the education which will reveal and generate his capabilities, he is termed "under-privileged," "from a deprived background," and everyone commiserates over the loss of a human's potential. "Oh, what proper training could have done for him!"

The Jew who does not receive a Torah education has similarly been deprived of the means which he needs to reach his fullest potential. As mentioned in the beginning, the Torah is the blueprint for the proper building of a Jew's life. Although he has nothing to do with his *creation*, the Jew has every-thing to do with his *re-creation*. In other words, the Torah and the Jew are a planned complement for the perfection of the human personality. Learn-ing Torah and performing mitzvot, the Jew com-pletes the purpose not only of his own existence but also of the existence of the whole world.

The Jew is different and everybody knows it. Some hide from this reality, some ignore it, some make excuses. He was created specially by the Creator to fulfill his particular function, and that function is different from that of any other human being. Everything else in life has a distinct role. A stone becomes part of a wall, a plant produces vegetables, a cow gives milk, a steelworker rivets pieces of metal, a doctor forms a cast on a broken bone. The Jew elevates all of the physical world to its highest spiritual potential. *Nobody else* has this mission — only the Jew. And he can do this assign-ment *only* through following the "building" in-structions in the Torah.

Now that the Jew realizes that he is special, distinct and unique, it follows *a fortiori* that if he does anything that thwarts the development of his particular potential, he is cutting his own throat. He is depriving himself of the opportunity to com-plete the task for which he was created. It is not enough to say such a result is a "shame." Rather say that it is plain senselessness.

Beyond a shadow of doubt, then, if a Jew decides to follow a life pattern other than the specific one given him, he is wasting his time in a vain and self-defeating venture. He needs a size 44 suit, and instead he is trying on a diaper. Utter nonsense. But that is the power which Hashem gives the Jew to make mistakes and live his own free choice.

Should a potential disease-preventing immunologist, for want of proper education and opportunity, end up as a ticket seller in a movie house, the loss to the world is infinitesimally insignificant compared to the loss when a Jew opts for any so-called religion, "trip" or life-style other than Torah and mitzvot.

So the Torah Jew is distressed and saddened when he hears that another Jew has gone off the track, whatever channel he has fallen into. True, the detour may not be his fault, for lack of education or miseducation. But in any case, it is one less vital beam in the house of the Jewish People, *all* of whom are needed to build the perfect world.

And how many times more worse is the case of intermarriage! Not only does the current generation lose a vital Jewish personality, but the deprivation continues for generations. When the male partner is Jewish, he has effectively cut himself off from the destiny and purpose of the Jewish People, thereby commiting his own eternal suicide. When the female partner is Jewish, the children are so weakened by the mixture that it is more than likely that they or the generation after them will be lost to the Jewish mission.

When a nation uncovers a vital resource within

its borders, it ensures by every means possible that it be preserved and properly used for the national benefit. Every Jew is a vital resource for the Jewish People in order that it perform its function of perfecting the world. When the Jews are together, they will succeed, says Hashem. When they act in a way that maximizes their joint potential, the world moves closer to its completion. When the Jew falters, drifts away, ignores his special role, then the world stays mired in its desperate plight.

XXIII

POLITICS AND PEACE

Everyone is an armchair political analyst, and everyone has his solution for world peace. Conferences are held, reports are filed, books are written, endless miles of newspaper are printed, millions upon millions of words are expended on how humans should run the world.

One would think, after all the experience of history, after all the combined efforts of human intelligence and sensitivity, after all the reform movements and study papers, that the world would now be only a step away from true peace. The reality, however, is just the opposite: it is a step away from its complete destruction.

The reason for this crisis is on the front page of every newspaper. Hashem the Creator is not mentioned in any of the articles. Important events, gripping issues, in-depth analyses — all ignore the Master Planner as if to say that the servant is running the show instead of the King. Of course, since western culture views the human as the master, this exclusion is no wonder. Nor, consequently, the sorry state of things.

Quite naturally, there is a high percentage of Jews involved in trying to remedy conditions. As discussed, in search of truth and purpose, they strive for a better world, a task certainly inspiring, yet sufficiently indefinite not to discourage them by the futility of their efforts. "But is not one small light better than cursing..."

Or is it?

Certainly there are successes, but these just lure people into thinking that the solution is always in fixing something out "there" — Congress, the U.N., international cartels, corrupt politicians, an insensitive bureaucracy...

Is there really anything new in any of the problems? Are the solutions ones unimagined or untried before? Has anything actually changed in the human dilemma?

Yet, tilting at the windmill, the valiant ones fight on (literally or from their armchairs), convinced that if they just keep struggling, then peace and truth will somehow arrive. Further, rushing to plug up the dike in its never-ending breaches, they can be well-occupied and well-satisfied that they are doing all that they can. Ironically, these herculean efforts all seem a bit macabre, if not absurd, when an aerial view shows, further upstream, a hundred-meter dam that is just about ready to burst.

Consistent with his death myopia, the individual ignores the imminent threat of the world's nuclear destruction, playing like a Pollyanna in a gazebo while six thousand python snakes curl ever so steadily through the latticework. No matter. With his tinted sunglasses, they look like garden snakes. After all, "what will be, will be, and what can I do about it anyway?"

But, at least, let him avoid a basic deception. He should not fool himself into thinking that he is bringing about world peace and the betterment of mankind when in the next second, by everyone's admission, the whole thing may go up in smoke. "Well, in the meantime, I'm doing a good job, aren't I?"

TORAH ON PEACE

Peace to the Torah Jew is not something out "there" but very much something inside. Were it that peace filled the whole world but was lacking within one individual, then peace would not fill the whole world. If the individual works on peace for all mankind and does not achieve it within himself, what has he gained?

Even accepting that helping others is an integral part of self-improvement and that a process directed to such a goal is not invalid just because it is difficult to achieve, we find that, *for the Jew*, no system other than Torah allows him to perfect the totality of his personality, effectuating a harmony of all the forces within him.

For example, in his effort to make the world better, a certain individual distributes food to poor people, regularly visits the aged, and is a foster father to orphan children. Quite meritorious, and a person to be emulated. But he also has some "small" problems: he becomes involved with other women besides his wife; he gets very angry if he feels insulted; he cannot help bearing grudges; he feels insecure unless he has money in the bank. Along with these, there is a constant nagging inside him: somehow he does not feel whole, somehow he is not really sure that all that he is doing has permanent value. He knows that he must help, but what does it all actually mean? So tomorrow there will be more unfortunate cases. On and on, and for what?

Torah was given to the Jew to complete him in *all* the many facets of life. No aspect of life is neglected; no problem area left without helpful guidance and corrective means. Through constantly doing the mitzvot, the Jew rehabilitates his behavior pattern above his "natural," more base instincts. Every part of him can become refined, purged of the impure dross. Indeed, Hashem purposely increased the number of the mitzvot so that all the different Jews with all their various weaknesses would have the tools to perfect themselves.

After all the words used to describe how Torah operates, perhaps a summary diagram will better describe the whole picture. The Torah Jew is encompassed by six intersecting planes that involve, channel and improve his entire existence (*see diagram on the following page*).

The integration of all these factors is the aim of Torah so that the Jew will achieve peace. Only the

Jew has this potential because only he is totally involved in Torah. Others may malign him, they may beat him, they may torture and slay him. But on him rest the hopes of the entire world. The dreaded expression "the final solution of the Jewish problem" is — in exactly the opposite way — true. The Jew is the final solution of the world's problem. Those who reject this principle and seek to

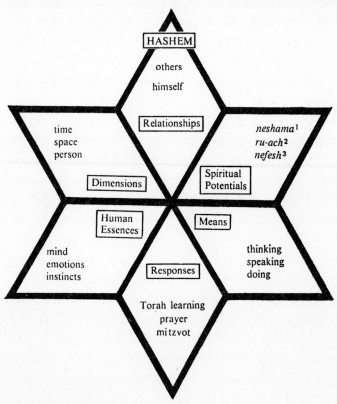

1. upper-world energy force
2. human energy force
3. physical energy force

harm or convert Jews are destroying themselves. History shows that every single adversary of the Jews has been undone, and the Jew still lives on. The Jew is eternal because his job is the purpose of creation, and Hashem is patient until he completes it.

Because the Jew himself sometimes runs away from his all-important mission, Hashem lets the detractors of the Jewish people do their mischief. When the Jew turns from Hashem and His Torah, he is moving contrary to his best interests, right into trouble, a blind alley, a dead end. And those who cause the trouble are only carrying out Hashem's will so that the Jew will change from the wrong way and return to the right path. Very simple, but sometimes very tragic.

XXIV

THE HOLOCAUST

For many reasons, Jews today want to avoid the whole topic of the Holocaust. After all, it is extremely upsetting and gruesome, and why be morbid when life in general is going so pleasantly? Besides, "it's over, it happened to others; it didn't happen to me."

Most of those who were in any direct way affected by it are also silent. It is better forgotten; certainly Jews are not by nature prone to dwell on tragedies. What purpose would be gained? Who can understand why?

Many use the Holocaust as a proof that Hashem does not exist, does not care or is too cruel for words.

And, finally, since for some the Holocaust has also become an academic study, when the discussions ignore Hashem it is as if all the learning has been in silence, without grasping the central point.

205

Racial-religious prejudices, socio-economic analyses, mass psychology are all just so many sand castles that wash away because, in the end, they really do not explain anything.

A TORAH VIEW OF THE HOLOCAUST

The last holocaust is only the most recent in a long line of holocausts, ones in which even far higher percentages than one third were lost. When the Jews left slavery in Egypt, eighty percent of the Jewish people were killed. When the Ten Tribes of the Northern Kingdom of Israel were vanquished and dragged into exile, only two tribes of Jews remained. When the Romans sacked Jerusalem and ravaged the Jews for centuries, only a small remnant of Jews lived on. When the Saracens chopped off the heads of the "non-believers" and the Crusaders impaled innocent women and children, whole Jewish communities were decimated throughout Europe, Northern Africa and the Middle East. When the pogroms were popular amusements in Europe, the Jew was a constant murder victim.

Of course, one photograph showing the absolute depravity and barbarity of the last holocaust would still convince one that it was the worst. But that it is one of a long list tells the Torah Jew the true significance of the event.

The Jewish People represent the building of a revolutionary world where death does not exist, where the human is completely one and whole with the Source of his creation, knowing no blockages between his self and the Self that is in total command. When each Jew strives to achieve this revolutionary world, then the power of death is diminished. When, unfortunately, he does not so strive, the power of death is increased.

Notice that *each Jew* is involved. The Jewish People are actually one unit with each person responsible for the others. All Jews are supposed to be pulling the rope. If one does not pull his load, then the others have it harder and can even be hurt. There are no bystanders in this drama because, when the rope goes, even those on the side can be caught in the momentum of the people falling, particularly since the unity of the Jewish People inextricably binds each Jew with his fellow — even if he is not so interested in the connection. Circumstances will ultimately force him to be attached to his true identity. One can hide from the police, but not from oneself.

Thus, the Holocaust is yet another demonstration that the Jews are not *together* doing the job which they were created to do. If the lesson remains ignored, then, unfortunately, most are familiar with what happens to the man who does not learn from history.

XXV

ISRAEL

Most would admit that this drama of human history has no point in going on indefinitely. More of the same failings and vanities brings no real benefit. Of course, the Jews who pass their tests and improve themselves make the continuation of the whole world worthwhile. But for the Jewish People as a whole to pass the test seems to be quite difficult.

As history moves to its final scenes, obviously the peak climax seems to be approaching: the Holocaust; the development of the atom and hydrogen bombs; the large return of the Jews to their ancient homeland, the Land of Israel; the flexing muscles of the raw-resource nations and the proliferation of nuclear weapons; the delicate balance of terror between the deadly giants. And, literally, right in the middle of everything is the Jew.

Unfortunately, many look at such events as

something distant or divorced from their lives. Concerning Israel, some admire the courage and endurance of those who happen to live in Israel. After all, even after the Holocaust, it is still an acceptable practice to shed Jewish blood. (How quickly the nations of the world forget!) But the principal views of Israel are as a nice tourist vacation spot —in and out of buses at forty-two different places in two weeks; a passive point of pride that Jews are not being kicked around without at least kicking back; a matter of concern when any trouble flares up; and, of course, a worthy cause for a yearly donation.

This middle position is flanked by both extremes: those who feel so committed to Israel that they willingly expend their time and energies to help it prosper and those who feel that Israel is making such mistakes that they endeavor to either block or redirect its progress. Such diversity of opinion is a Jewish trait and, therefore, to be expected. Since prophecy no longer exists, it is impossible to see the future with any clarity. But any position that views Israel without considering the past is missing the crucial lesson that it presents to the Jew and to the nations of the world.

Some salient facts:

— six million Jews are murdered in Europe and a scattered remnant seeks a refuge where perhaps they can live unmolested.

— the western nations create a "United Nations" that is supposed to keep civil what is left of

civilization after World War II. The only time
that the great powers agree on a major political
issue in the U.N. is the partition of Palestine.

— with hundreds of thousand square miles to live
in, the Arab states cannot tolerate the existence
of a handful of Jews in an area far less than
one percent of their size — an area in which
everyone agrees Jews have historical claims and
have continually lived for thousands of years.

— against ridiculously impossible odds, the Jews
are granted both victory and more territory —
not just once, but several times.

— a small but crucial amount of American Jewish
influence combines with United States self-in-
terest to give Israel some support in a world
which would prefer that it not exist.

— deprived of military victory, the Arabs are given
the car keys to drive the motorized western civilization to a grinding halt.

— the powder keg on which the whole world sits
is most ignitable in the Middle East, particularly since, most probably, both Israel and the
Arabs have some measure of nuclear capability.

It does not take a particularly clairvoyant person
to see that something very important — even mon-
umental — is about to happen.

TORAH AND ISRAEL

Hashem gave the Jews the Land of Israel so that they would have a special place to carry out the unique mission for which He created them. The non-Jews have countries that are sources of national pride and glorification. The Jew possesses the Land of Israel not to glorify himself but to glorify Hashem. If all the peoples of the world would see the Jewish People living as a unit in its homeland and serving the Creator according to the way that He directed, then they would realize what the purpose of life is and how to accomplish it. The Jew is supposed to be the model for the individual. When he is together as a People in his homeland, he is a model for all the nations as well.

Once these principles are understood, the following conclusions are readily comprehensible:

When the Jew is in Israel and he does not live in the Land according to Hashem's will, he can expect considerable harassment and difficulties.* After all, the continued possession of any conditional gift depends on the fulfillment of the conditions. (Perhaps now it is a little clearer why, having established its sovereignty on purely nationalistic claims, Israel must now combat the equally presentable, though erroneous, nationalistic claims of others.)

Now that this unusual confluence of events has initiated the physical rebirth and regrowth of the Jewish People in its homeland, an opportunity beyond comparison exists for the Jew to use the special powers which Hashem has granted him in the very place where Hashem intended originally that he activate them.

Because the world has reached the combustion point of self-annihilation with a time-fuse in Israel, the pressure is clearly on the Jew to realize that all these events are happening solely so that he should return to Hashem and His Torah before it is too late, not only for him but also for the whole world. Likewise, the non-Jews should realize that this may be their last opportunity either to support the People of Israel or to be destroyed like all the enemies of the Jews in the past.

The Jew on the side, who does not care to be involved in all these issues, is risking his life. No

* While certainly we pray daily for the cessation of hostilities in the Middle East, no one should imagine that, thereby, "peace" will come. As explained in Chapter XXIII, peace depends on character improvement and closeness to Hashem — both for the Jew as an individual and as a nation.

Jew can escape. No Jew can hide. No Jew can say that it is not his responsibility. He is the *only one* who has the potential to save the world. And if he pretends that it is none of his business, then like the German Jews before and during World War II, he will find that the non-Jews will very soon remind him of his Jewishness. If, instead, the Jews take the offense and strive to follow their unique destiny as the servants of Hashem and His Torah, then they will no longer be on the defense, vulnerable, uncertain and drifting. The challenge is now clear. The Jew can change the world in a moment. He just has to want to. He just has to want to return to Hashem.

CONCLUSION

Only someone who wants to be convinced can be convinced. Every single presentation in this book can be rebutted by a plausible counter-argument. The free choice that Hashem gives the Jew requires that there be at least two sides to every issue — otherwise there is no choice. Each reader will make his own decision whether from now on he wants to be more Jewish, to find out more about Hashem and His Torah.

This book's purpose is to spur the Jew on to achieve his special role in life, a role that no other human being has. Down deep in each Jew, there is the desire to fulfill his unique identity. If he is not too busy with other things and is not afraid to sit alone in a room and ask himself who he really is, then maybe this book can convince him that there is something more to life than he had thought, that maybe being more of a Jew is more important than he had realized.

Of course, up until this moment there may have been a hundred excuses why he has not been interested. But he should not be trapped by his past; he should not say "it is too late" or "how can I change now" or "what difference does it make." No. Every step, however small, to intensify his Jewishness is absolutely crucial. Ever so gradually, a whole new world of living can open for him, allowing him to experience, for the first time, that fullness of life which Hashem originally planned for him. The reader should not feel uncomfortable if, perhaps, he was convinced a little. Who knows? After he starts learning about Torah and mitzvot, maybe he will be far more persuasive in helping other Jews come to Hashem.

Practical Applications

Since Torah is a plan of revolutionary action, it would be inappropriate for this book to conclude without proposing some practical suggestions to the reader. Like everything else that is so different for the Torah Jew, reading a book is not just a nice way to fill spare time. If the person is not any different when he finished the book from when he started, why did he bother reading it in the first place? There is no time to waste in this short life.

The older reader
For the Jew who has established a set life-style over many years, it is extremely difficult to open

up to the Torah way of life. Being comfortable, being satisfied, being habituated are just part of the problem. The real issue is the lifetime intellectual and emotional commitment to a certain way of thinking. Right or wrong — that is the approach which the person has, and his equilibrium will not tolerate any major changes. In self-defense, he cannot afford to say or even think that his whole life (or the great proportion of it) has been wrong, misdirected, wasted.

This Jew should not feel bad in the slightest. What is past is past; from this day onward he can make a new slate, a fresh start. In fact, if he sincerely wants now to maximize his Jewishness, all his life is considered as if he had followed his new pattern.

And what is this new pattern? In five words: studying Torah and doing mitzvot. At every age, in every location, under any conditions,* all that the Jewish man or woman has to do in order to understand what it really means to be Jewish is to learn Torah and how it is put into practice (the mitzvot).** He must also learn not just from anybody

---

* No reader should feel intimidated by his lack of knowledge, nor should he worry about learning Hebrew texts. Today, many of the primary Torah books are translated into English. Moreover, with steady application, the reader will speedily master a basic Hebrew facility.
** Although we have provided a list of Torah books suitable for beginners (see Appendix B), the prime method of learning Torah is through *relationships*. Therefore, the reader should not be content with just reading books, but should endeavor to establish a

but only from a rav who himself believes in and practices Torah.* Otherwise, he could be involved in an academic endeavor that will not grip him personally and emotionally.

Once the Jew has found a Torah teacher, he will be directed on the exact course of learning suited to his particular intelligence, sensitivities and background. At whatever age and level, there is Torah which he can learn and mitzvot which he can do. The only question is how much time and interest he has. This book has tried to make the western-culture Jew aware that there is *nothing* more worthwhile for him than to take the time and interest in order to learn Torah. More money he does not need; most entertainments are already boring. So use the many hours still left in life to learn.

Young adult Jews

The reader who is just beginning or is in the midst of his success climb is not likely to have a spare moment, except for needed relaxation. This Jew, already geared and trained to measure his life in terms of western-culture progress, must ask himself this one question: "What makes me different from my non-Jewish co-worker?"

When he finds that, in substance, there is no real difference in their high level work production,

learning association with a Torah-observant personality. (Cf. Chapter X.)
* See Appendix C.

occupational commitment, enjoyments and life-style, he may just realize that something very important is missing in his life — his Jewishness. Then he might decide to stop his copying of the "Joneses" and take time out of his schedule to learn how to make a truly unique contribution to the world scene.

College people

The time to experiment, to test new and old theories, to open new avenues of thought, to grow intensively in the face of difficult challenges — here are those magic college years, which will soon become such fond memories (except for final exam time!).

"But wait a minute. Nobody's talking to *me*. I'm not a 15th century Renaissance Italian. I'm not a test tube filled with chemicals. I'm not merely a robot, trained to ingest and churn out data, consuming energy and ejecting pollution. I'm *me*. I'm a Jew. Why does everyone avoid the topic or approach it with such disdain? And why does everything they say about being Jewish sound so distant, colorless, unappealing? I have 3300 years of the richest and most profound culture in the world, and all they're telling me about is imperial dynasties, third-generation computers, Hegelian dialectic and double-helix chromosomes. Hold it a second. Teach me something about *me*."

In reality, they will never teach for the Jew because they could not care less. And if what is called

Jewish education is not being taught by a rav who believes Torah and practices mitzvot himself, then it is all a game of who knows more information in order to please the teacher and pass the exams.

Still, many young college Jews innately sense that learning more about their Jewish selves is what will bring them greater satisfaction and self-awareness. They choose college subjects in religion, philosophy and psychology. They enjoy reading the whole range of paperback books that discuss Judaism, the art of giving and the search for meaning. They write and publish Jewish magazines, newsletters and catalogues. Some even take part-time courses off-campus in Torah institutions.

But the larger percentage is so busy with papers, tests and the college scene that they have little time to delve into Torah and the real Jewish experience. The answer to the problem is to take a leave of absence for a year or two and come to the places where Torah is taught especially for such college people.* Leaves of absence today have become both popular and acceptable. Even parents approve. The free time and energy to come face-to-face with the truth about being a Jew will not be just a refreshing opportunity. It will be like water in a wasteland.

---

* See Appendix A. Many of these new yeshivot for beginners are suited for people from age 18 to 35 and over. Further, those who have some Jewish background or are already involved in Jewish studies can find in these yeshivot the true environment to improve and advance their full Jewish potential.

High school readers

Many sensitive young Jews feel early a strong identity crisis. What they are taught about Judaism has so little to do with their lives and daily experiences that it offers no help in their struggles. They depend heavily on parents and teachers to guide them in their searchings. Wherever they are led, they do their best to comprehend and incorporate a personal meaning. Yet at this juncture in their lives, everything is tentative, without final decisions or commitments.

Still, for these readers perhaps this book has sparked a new insistence to know the truth about being Jewish. Perhaps they will venture a bit more courageously on their own to find the real sources of Judaism. Perhaps they will respectfully dissent and proclaim their disappointment at the lack of real values and positive direction in their lives. Perhaps they will insist that their Jewish identities are crying for nourishment and all that they are being given is a few artificial sugar pills.

Parents with school-children

If it were not for the children who learn Torah, there would be no Jewish People, because without education the next generation cannot possibly know what it means to be Jewish.

Jewish parents of all persuasions realize this need and almost always make an effort to provide some Jewish education. But if the parents want their children to know the truth about being Jewish, and

221

not a watered-down misrepresentation, they will send them to Torah schools, which are located in almost every city. At the same time, the parents should also learn on a part-time basis so that the new Jewish knowledge and way of life which the children bring home will have both an open and a willing reception. The first step in learning to become more Jewish is to admit ignorance and, then, not to be afraid when others — even children — contribute to revealing truth.

Remember, all beginnings are difficult, but with sincere effort each Jew and his family can reap a harvest of blessing beyond their most creative imaginations.

The non-category Jew

For the Jew who makes it his business not to fit into any categories, this book will not find favor. Too straight, too simple, too organized. Particularly if every Jew is supposed to be doing the same thing (Torah and mitzvot), he will not tolerate his individuality being crushed in the crowd. It is better to go his own way than to compromise his independence.

Early in this book we discussed the importance of giving one's supposed independence back to Hashem in order to gain true independence. But nothing has been mentioned of yet another basic principle: individuality.

No two Jews are exactly alike, and the particular way that each serves Hashem is unique to him.

Every Jew does all the mitzvot, but the proportion, balance and emphasis are special for each person.

Indeed, Hashem created each Jew to do a specific function within the total mission of the Jewish People. Nobody else can do that specific function, only the one designated. And how peaceful a person can feel when he knows that he is fulfilling his distinctive portion in life.

So, the non-category Jew should take heart. There is plenty of room for him too if only he wants to learn how Torah can refine and complete his individuality.

The "frum" reader

If this book has succeeded in expressing the absolute truth which you represent, please do not let it sit on your library shelf. Lend it out to any interested Jew who does not yet know the true meaning of being Jewish — and discuss it with him afterwards.

Why? Because your Judaism is affected by and depends on the level and intensity of every Jew's Judaism. You can never be completely content until the truth which you live is shared and built together with every other Jew. If the task sounds difficult, then you are appreciating the challenge and responsibility of being Jewish.

הֲשִׁיבֵנוּ ה׳ אֵלֶיךָ וְנָשׁוּבָה; חַדֵּשׁ יָמֵינוּ כְּקֶדֶם.

APPENDIX A

Some of the new yeshivoth (Torah schools) for beginners

(listed alphabetically; please inform the publishers of corrections and additions)

KEY
M:Men   W:Women
M/W: Separate divisions
  for men and for women
E: English   H: Hebrew
F: French   R: Russian
*Special rural Torah-study
communities for families

Telephone numbers are given
in parentheses

AISH HA TORAH
Rechov Chayei Olam
P.O.B. 14149
Jewish Quarter
The Old City
Jerusalem, Israel
M E   (284182)

Also:
12411 Chandler Blvd.
North Hollywood,
California 91607
(Rabbi Zvi Block)
(980-6934)

986 Warder Avenue
St. Louis, Missouri 63130
(Rabbi Kalman Packouz)
(721-9222)

3888 Bathurst St.
Apt. 105
Toronto, Canada
(Rabbi Benjamin Karan)
(782-2174)
(633-8333)

BAIS YISROEL
TORAH CENTER
1821 Ocean Parkway
Brooklyn, NY 11223
(Rabbi Avigdor Miller)
M/W E (336-8252)

CHICAGO INSTITUTE/
TELSHE YESHIVA (C.I.T.Y.)
3535 W. Foster Ave.
Chicago, Illinois 60625
M E (463-7738)

DARCHE NOAM
Sara Schenirer
Special Program
5218 16th Avenue
Brooklyn, NY 11204
W E (438-2349)

225

DIASPORA YESHIVA
Har Zion/P.O.B. 6426
Jerusalem, Israel
M/W EH (716841)

DVAR YERUSHALAYIM/
JERUSALEM ACADEMY OF
JEWISH STUDIES
Rechov HaYeshiva 8
Geulah/P.O.B. 5454
Jerusalem, Israel
M/W EHFR* (288645)

Also:
506 East 7th Street
Brooklyn, NY 11218
(Rabbi Mordechai Potash)
(284-8836)

7 Highcroft Gardens
London NW11, England
(Rabbi Dr. J. Freilich)
M/W E (455-8631)

96 Greenlea Road
Terenure, Dublin 6
Ireland
(Mr. Sefton Yodaikon)
(909-258)

Stenecourt Synagogue,
Holden Road,
Salford 7, Lancs.
Manchester, England
(Rev. G. Brodie)
(740-2586)

HA MAAYAN
P.O.B. 155
Beer-Sheva, Israel
(Rabbi Nathan Spector)
M/W EH (73667)

HAMIVTAR
Sederot Hameiri 11
Jerusalem, Israel
M/W EH (535312)

Also:
MICHLELET BRURIA
Rechov Ben-Zion 19
Jerusalem, Israel

THE HEBREW
THEOLOGICAL COLLEGE
(Beginners Program)
7135 N. Carpenter Rd.
Skokie, Illinois 60076
(Rabbi Well)
M E

KEREM YESHIVAH
250 Howard Drive
Santa Clara, CA
(Rabbi Matis Weinberg)
M E (247-1722)

KFAR CHABAD
Kfar Chabad, Israel
M EH (704327)

THE KOLLEL
(Beginners Program)
48 Urania Street
Observatory, Johannesburg
South Africa

_____

KOLLEL BAIS AVRAHAM
7561 Beverly Boulevard
Los Angeles, CA
(Special English Torah Library)
(933-7193)

_____

MAGEN AVRAHAM
Rechov Chatam Sofer 8
Bnei Brak, Israel
M E   (703100)

_____

MELBOURNE COMMUNITY
YESHIVAH CENTRE KOLLEL
c/o 92 Hotham Street
East St. Kilda
Victoria, Australia
M EHR

_____

MIGDAL TORAH
Cong. Bais Shalom
Jersey & Hollywood Sts.
Chicago, Illinois
(Rabbi Heisler and
Rabbi Levitansky)

_____

MIKDASH MELECH
1326 Ocean Parkway
Brooklyn, NY 11230

_____

THE NEW ENGLAND
CHASSIDIC CENTER
1710 Beacon Street
Brookline, Massachusetts

_____

N'VEI YERUSHALAYIM
Rechov Cassuto 5
Bayit Vegan
Jerusalem, Israel
W EHF (424227)

_____

OHAVEI TORAH
c/o Rechov Rashi 11
Bnei Brak, Israel
(Rabbi S. Weisman)
M E (792673)

_____

OHEL CHANA COLLEGE
for Advanced Jewish
Studies
88 Hotham Street
Balaclava, Victoria
Australia
(Rabbi T. Aron)
W E

_____

OHR SOMAYACH
Rechov Shimon HaTzaddik 22
P.O.B. 18103
Jerusalem, Israel
M/W EH*   (810315)

Also:
112 S'deroth Rothschild
Tel Aviv, Israel
(Rabbi Grelack)
M E/H   (226820)

152 Rechov Herzl
Rehovot, Israel
(Rabbi Zvi Schwartz)
M H   (57395)

142 Route 306
P.O.B. 334
Monsey, NY 10952
(Mr. E. Shapiro)
(356-2158)

RABBINICAL COLLEGE OF
AUSTRALIA & NEW ZEALAND
67 Alexandra Avenue
East St. Kilda
Victoria, Australia 3183
(Rabbi Benyomin Cohen)
M E

RABBINICAL SEMINARY
OF AMERICA
(Preparatory Program)
92-15 69th Avenue
Forest Hills, NY 11375
(Rabbi Mines)

SHAPELL COLLEGE
OF JEWISH STUDIES
see Yeshivat Darche Noam

SH'OR YOSHUV YESHIVA
Rabbinical College/
Institute for Jewish Studies
1526 Central Avenue
Far Rockaway, NY 11691
M E   (327-2048)

Also:
AYELET HASHACHAR
Women's Teachers'
Seminary & Institute for
Jewish Studies
702 Bolton Road
Far Rockaway, NY 11691
W E

YESHIVA DERECH CHAIM
4907 18th Avenue
Brooklyn, NY 11204
M E

YESHIVA PRI ZADIK
1089 Coney Island Ave.
Brooklyn, NY
M E   (434-3041)

YESHIVAH COLLEGE CENTRE
— MELBOURNE
92 Hotham Street
Victoria, Australia
(Rabbi I. D. Groner)
M/W E

YESHIVAH COLLEGE
— SYDNEY
36 Flood Street
Bondi, NSW 2
Australia

YESHIVAT DARCHE NOAM/
SHAPELL COLLEGE
OF JEWISH STUDIES
Rechov HaOhr 2
P.O.B. 13209
Jerusalem, Israel
M E   (521884)

Also:
1239 East 8th Street
Brooklyn, New York
(338-3400)

___

YESHIVAT TIFERES
BACHURIM
(Lubavitch-Chabad)
226 Sussex Avenue
Morristown,
New Jersey 07960
M E

Also contact:
770 Eastern Parkway
Brooklyn, NY 12213
(Rabbi K. Kastel)
(PR 8-9270)

HADAR HA TORAH
824 Eastern Parkway
Brooklyn, NY 11213
M E (778-4600)

MACHON CHANA
733 Eastern Parkway
Brooklyn, NY 11213
W E   (735-0217)

BAIS CHANA FOR GIRLS
15 Montcalm Court
St. Paul, Minnesota 55116
W E

CHABAD HOUSE
1930 Vine Street
Berkeley, California
(Rabbi C. Drizin)

___

Rabbi Gedalia Fleer
1738 East 4th Street
Brooklyn, NY 11225
M/W E

___

APPENDIX B

Some of the Torah literature available for beginners

A Woman of Valour: An Anthology for the Thinking Jewess. London: Lubavitch Foundation, 1976

Carmell, Aryeh & Domb, Cyril, eds., *Challenge: Torah Views on Science and Its Problems.* Jerusalem: Feldheim Publishers, 1978

Cohn, Jacob, *The Royal Table (the Jewish dietary laws).* Jerusalem: Feldheim Publishers, 1970

Culi, Yaakov, *The Torah Anthology (Me'am Lo'ez),* translated by Aryeh Kaplan. New York/Jerusalem: Maznaim Publishing Corp., 1977

Dessler, Eliyahu, *Strive for Truth,* rendered into English by Aryeh Carmell. Jerusalem: Feldheim Publishers, 1978

Donin, Chaim, *To Be a Jew.* New York: Basic Books, 1976

Eisenberg, Rafael, *A Matter of Return.* Jerusalem: Feldheim Publishers, 1980

Fendel, Zechariah, *Anvil of Sinai; Challenge of Sinai.* New York: Hashkafah Publications, 1977, 1978

Gevirtz, Eliezer, *Lehavin Ul'haskil.* New York: JEP Publications, distributed by Feldheim, 1980

Grunfeld, Dayan Dr. I., *The Sabbath,* Jerusalem: Feldheim Publishers, 1972

Halevi, Judah, *The Kuzari.* New York: Schocken Books, 1971

Hirsch, Samson Raphael, *The Nineteen Letters.* Jerusalem: Feldheim Publishers, 1969

——— *The Hirsch Siddur* with commentary. Jerusalem: Feldheim Publishers, 1972

Katz, Mordechai, *Lilmod Ul'lamade.* New York: JEP Publications, distributed by Feldheim, 1978

Kitov, Eliyahu, *The Book of Our Heritage (the cycle of the Jewish year),* translated by Nathan Bulman. Jerusalem: Feldheim Publishers, 1972

——— *The Jew and His Home,* translated by Nathan Bulman. New York: Shengold Publishers, 1976

Lamm, Norman, *A Hedge of Roses* (on family purity). New York: Feldheim Publishers, 1972

Lehmann, Marcus, *The Passover Hagadah* with commentary, London: Honigson Publishing Co., 1969

Meiseles, Meir, *Judaism: Thought and Legend*. Jerusalem/New York: Feldheim Publishers, 1977

Miller, Avigdor, *Rejoice O Youth; Behold a People; Torah Nation*. New York

Munk, Eli, *The Seven Days of the Beginning*. Jerusalem/New York: Feldheim Publishers, 1974 (for more advanced beginners)

Packouz, Kalman, *How to Stop an Intermarriage*. Jerusalem: 1976

Pliskin, Zelig, *Guard Your Tongue*. Jerusalem, 1975

——— *Love Thy Neighbor*. Jerusalem, 1978

Posner, Zalman, *Think Jewish*. Nashville: Kesher Press, 1979

Raz, Simcha, *A Tzaddik in Our Time*, translated by Charles Wengrov. Jerusalem: Feldheim Publishers, 1976

Schiller, Mayer, *The Road Back*. Jerusalem: Feldheim Publishers, 1976

Sefer haHinnuch, translated by Charles Wengrov. Vol. I: Genesis-Exodus. Jerusalem: Feldheim Publishers, 1978

Siddur (Prayer Book): *The Hafetz Hayyim on the Siddur*, translated by Charles Wengrov. Jerusalem: Feldheim Publishers, 1974

Tanach (Bible): *The ArtScroll Tanach Series*. New York: Mesorah Publications (text, translation and commentary on Books of the Torah, Prophets and Writings).

The Spice and Spirit of Jewish Cooking. Brooklyn: Lubavitch Women's Organization, Junior Division, 1977

Wouk, Herman, *This Is My God*. Doubleday Publishing Co., 1973

Publications from the National Conference of Synagogue Youth, 116 East 27th Street, New York, NY 10016:

Kaplan, Aryeh, *God, Man and Tefillin*

——— *Shabbos — Day of Eternity*

——— *Love Means Reaching Out*

——— *The Mystery of the Mikveh*

Kornreich, Yaakov, ed., *A Science and Torah Reader*

——— *The Real Messiah*

Stolper, Pinchas, *What Happened on Sinai*.

——— *The Road to Responsible Jewish Adulthood*

APPENDIX C
List of Rabbis

The rabbis listed herein are generally known to represent authentic Torah values and would probably be available to answer and discuss any questions. This list is not exclusive nor, except for several rabbis known to the author, has it been personally verified. The following are sincerely thanked for their kind assistance in compiling this list: Rabbi Kalman Packouz (from his original list in *How to Stop an Intermarriage*), Rabbi Gavriel Beer and his son Zvi, Mrs. Rachel Wise (Rabbinical Council of America) and students of the Mirrer Yeshivah, Jerusalem, particularly Eli Lichtman.

ALABAMA

Rabbi Moshe Stern
c/o Knesset Israel
3225 Montevalo Road
Birmingham 35210

ARIZONA

Rabbi Z. Levertov
915 W. 14th St., Tempe

CALIFORNIA

Rabbi C. I. Drizin
2340 Piedmont Ave., Berkeley

Rabbi E. Piekarski
3723 Lewis Ave., Long Beach

Rabbi S. Cunin
11058 Strathmore Dr., L.A.

Rabbi Pinchos Gruman
660 Spaulding Ave., L.A.

Rabbi Aaron Twersky
Cong. Netzach Israel
4117 Beverly Road, L.A.

Rabbi Zvi Bloch
5444 14th Place
North Hollywood

Rabbi Y. Lebovics
12803 Burbank Blvd.
North Hollywood

Rabbi Y. Fradkin
6115 Montezuma Rd.
San Diego

Rabbi P. Lipner
San Francisco

Rabbi D. Thaler
577 27th Ave., San Francisc

Rabbi Matis Weinberg
250 Howard Dr., Santa Cla

COLORADO

Rabbi Yaakov Hopfer
1375 Utica, Denver

Rabbi Nussi Lauer
Utica St., Denver

Rabbi Shlomo Melamed
1260 Sheridan, Denver

Rabbi Twersky
3800 14th Ave., Denver

Rabbi Y. Wasserman
1400 Quitman St., Denver

CONNECTICUT

Rabbi I. Stock
77 Mt. Pleasant Drive
Bridgeport-Trumbull

Rabbi Okolico
44 Chamberlain St.
New Britain

Rabbi Zalman Morosow
152 Groffe Ter., New Haven

Rabbi Mendy Gopin
Cong. Ahavas Chesed
New London

Rabbi Michell D. Geller
Cong. Brothers of Joseph
2 Broad St., Norwich

Rabbi M. Hecht
261 Derby Ave.
Orange

Rabbi Kenneth Auman
Stamford

FLORIDA

Rabbi D. Eliezrie
1540 Albenga Ave.
Coral Gables

Rabbi Chaim Segal
Miami

Rabbi A. Korf
1401 Alton Road, Miami Beach

Rabbi David Lehrfield
Cong. Knesseth Israel
1415 Euclid, Miami Beach

Rabbi S. B. Lipskare
3917 N. Meridan Ave.
Miami Beach

Rabbi Mordecai Shapiro
Beth Israel Cong.
770 W. 40th St., Miami Beach

Rabbi P. A. Weberman
5944 Pinetree Dr.
Miami Beach

Rabbi Israel Rivkin
Cong. Beth Moshe
3620 Fletcher Ave., Tampa

GEORGIA

Rabbi S. Bluming
1180 Biltmore Dr., Atlanta

Rabbi Emanuel Feldman
Cong. Beth Jacob
1855 La Vista Rd., N.E.
Atlanta

Rabbi B. Steifel
1168 Biltmore Dr. N.E.
Atlanta

Rabbi Chaim Capland
5543 Camelot Dr., Savannah

ILLINOIS

Rabbi Hershel Berger
2820 Sherwin St., Chicago

Rabbi Joseph Deitcher
525 W. Roscoe St., Chicago

Rabbi Chaim Keller
5437 N. St. Louis, Chicago

Rabbi D. Moscowitz
6136 N. Francisco, Chicago

Rabbi H. Shusterman
6227 N. Albany, Chicago

Rabbi Y. Eichenstein
6550 Troy, Skokie

IOWA

Rabbi M. B. Kasowitz
2932 University Ave., Des Moines

LOUISIANA

Rabbi Z. Rivkin
7037 Freret St.
New Orleans

Rabbi Eli Schepansky
New Orleans

MAINE

Rabbi C. Yaffee
94 Noyes St., Portland

MARYLAND

Rabbi Naftali Berg
3901 Clarinth Road, Baltimore

Rabbi Moshe Eisman
Rabbi Reuven Drucker
Rabbi Eliezer Gibber
Ner Israel Rabbinical Col.
400 Mt. Wilson Lane,
Baltimore

Rabbi S. Kaplan
5721 Park Hgts. Ave., Baltimore

Rabbi David Meister
6200 Gist Ave., Baltimore

Rabbi Herman N. Neuberger
401 Yeshiva Lane, Baltimore

Rabbi Joseph Schecter
3407 W. Strathmore Ave.
Baltimore

Rabbi Yaakov Weinberg
401 Yeshiva Lane, Baltimore

Rabbi M. Silverman
4812 B College Ave. 4B
College Park

Rabbi Gedalia Anemer
Yeshivah High School
University Blvd., Silver Spring

MASSACHUSETTS

Rabbi Y. Deren
30 N. Hadley Rd., Amherst

Rabbi M. Bergstein
46 Euston Road, Brighton

Rabbi Chaim Pruss
42 Kikwood Road, Brighton

Rabbi E. Wenger
38 Embassy Road, Brighton

Rabbi Levi Horowitz
1710 Beacon Street, Brookline

Rabbi Yehuda Kelemer
89 Pleasant St., Brookline

Rabbi Joseph Polak
60 Dwight St., Brookline

Rabbi Joseph B. Soloveitchik
10 Hancock Road, Brookline

Rabbi D. Wichnin
51 Cottage Farm Rd., Brookline

Rabbi D. Edelman
15 Elwood Dr., Springfield

Rabbi Y. Blotner
17 Kensington Rd., Worcester

Rabbi H. Fogelman
24 Creswell, Worcester

Rabbi Joseph Gold
43 Mitland St., Worcester

MICHIGAN

Rabbi A. Goldstein
715 Hill, Ann Arbor

Rabbi M. Avtzon
Vernon Ave., Oak Park

Rabbi Avraham Freedman
26135 Harding, Oak Park

Rabbi Shalom Goldstein
24610 Sussex, Oak Park

Rabbi James Gordon
Y.I. of Oak-Woods
Coolidge Hwy., Oak Park

Rabbi Y. M. Kagan
23080 Parklawn, Oak Park

Mr. Norman Levitin
14500 Sherwood, Oak Park

Rabbi S. B. Shem Tov
14000 W. 9 Mile Rd., Oak Park

Rabbi Chaim Silverstein
26040 Stratford Rd., Oak Park

Rabbi Felvel Wagner
Y.I. of Greenfield, Oak Park

Rabbi Morton E. Yolkut
24350 Southfield Rd.
Southfield

MINNESOTA

Dr. V. Greene
1601 N. Spring Valley Rd.
Minneapolis

Rabbi Nahum Schulman
2843 Raleigh Ave. South
Minneapolis

Rabbi M. Feller
15 Montcalm Ct., St. Paul

Rabbi A. Zeilengold
1731 Saunders St., St. Paul

MISSOURI

Rabbi Weinberg
8243 Virginia, Kansas City

Rabbi Yitzchak Kleiman
7901 Balson, St. Louis

NEBRASKA

Rabbi B. Garb
1513 N. 48th St. 38, Omaha

NEW JERSEY

Rabbi Yoseph Blau
Elizabeth

Rabbi Pinchas Teitz
Elizabeth

Rabbi Isaac Louis Swift
Cong. Ahavath Torah
240 Broad Ave. Englewood

Rabbi Y. Danziger
1004 Madison Ave., Lakewood

Rabbi Yosef Zimbal
Beit Midrash Govoah
617 6th St., Lakewood

Rabbi Steven M. Dworken
1605 Orchard Terrace, Linden

Rabbi Moshe A. Kasinetz
52 North Livingston Ave.
Livingston

Rabbi S. B. Gordon
12 Wellesley Road, Maplewood

Rabbi A. Lipsker
226 Sussex Ave., Maplewood

Rabbi S. Bogomilsky
250 Mt. Vernon Pl., Newark

Rabbi E. Carlbach
250 Williamson Ave., Newark

Rabbi N. Weinstein
P.O. Box 128, Norma

Rabbi Abraham I. Zigelman
Temple Beth Abraham
8410 Fourth Ave., North Bergen

Chaplain Lt. Col.
Max H. Daina
44 Fairfield Ave., Oceanport

Rabbi S. Bobrowsky
33 Ascension St., Passaic

Rabbi Chaim Davis
Yeshivah Mercaz Hatorah
Passaic

Rabbi M. Greenberg
6 Manor Rd., Patterson

Rabbi Y. Brod
41 Westgate Rd., Teaneck

Rabbi Macy A. Gordon
Cong. Bnai Yeshurun
641 W. Englewood Ave.
Teaneck

Rabbi Simon
2202 Sunset Ave., Wanamassa

Rabbi Herson
24 Schmitt Road, W. Orange

NEW YORK

Dr. Luchins
SUNY at Albany
53 Fordham Ct., Albany

Rabbi Y. Rubin
122 S. Main St., Albany

Rabbi Theodore Charner
Mid-Island Hebrew Day School
42 Locust Ave., Bethpage

Rabbi Jacob Bulka
Cong. K. Adath Yeshurun
2222 Cruger Ave., Bronx

Rabbi Zevulun Charlop
3231 Steuben Ave., Bronx

Rabbi David B. Hollander
1750 Grand Concourse, Bronx

Rabbi Maurice L. Schwartz
1375 Virginia Ave., Bronx

Rabbi Charles Sheer
2710 Edgehill Ave., Bronx

Rabbi Jacob Sodden
Van Cortland Jewish Center
3880 Sedgwick Ave., Bronx

Rabbi Yisroel Belsky
506 E. 7th St., Brooklyn

Rabbi E. Bluth
2080 77th St., Brooklyn

Rabbi Herbert W. Bomzer
1781 Ocean Pkwy., Brooklyn

Rabbi Alfred Cohen
105-14 Flatlands 4th St.
Brooklyn

Rabbi Solomon E. Drillman
956 East 54th St., Brooklyn

Rabbi Joseph M. Frankel
823 East 46th St., Brooklyn

Rabbi Avner G. German
Cong. B'nai Israel
859 Hendrix St., Brooklyn

Rabbi Jacob Greenberg
1464 E. 89th St., Brooklyn

Rabbi Abraham B. Hecht
Cong. Shaare Zion
2030 Ocean Pkwy., Brooklyn

Rabbi Jacob J. Hecht
824 Eastern Pkwy., Brooklyn

Rabbi Nochum Josephy
1163 47th St., Brooklyn

Rabbi Joseph Kaminetsky
1466 54 St., Brooklyn

Rabbi Kasriel Kastel
770 Eastern Pkwy., Brooklyn

Rabbi Leo Landman
Cong. Talmud Torah of Flatbush
1305 Coney Island Ave., Brooklyn

Rabbi Naftali M. Langsam
Shever Y'hudah Reznick
Institute of Technology
670 Rockaway Pkwy., Brooklyn

Rabbi Avigdor Miller
1821 Ocean Pkwy., Brooklyn

Rabbi Julius Parnes
970 50th St., Brooklyn

Rabbi Jacob M. Rabinowitz
1752 45th St., Brooklyn

Rabbi S. J. Sharfman
1012 Avenue I, Brooklyn

Rabbi Solomon B. Shapiro
Cong. B'nai Abraham
407 East 53 St., Brooklyn

Rabbi Gurary
3292 Main St., Buffalo

Rabbi Herman Eisner
Cong. Ezrath Yisroel
34 Center St., Ellenville

Rabbi Shlomo Freifeld
1526 Central Avenue
Far Rockaway

Rabbi Isaac M. Goodman
716 B. 9th St., Far Rockaway

Rabbi Chaim Feuerman
Yeshiva of Central Queens
90-40 150th St., Flushing

Rabbi Jacob Kleinman
75-26 169th St., Flushing

Rabbi Fabian Schonfeld
150-05 70th Rd., Flushing

Rabbi Morris Charner
Dov Revel Synagogue
70-02 113th St., Forest Hills

Rabbi J. A. Grunblatt
Queens Jewish Center
66-05 108th St., Forest Hills

Rabbi Marvin Luban
Yellowstone Blvd. & Burns
Forest Hills

Rabbi Hershel Solnica
Cong. Tifereth Israel
88th St. & 32nd Ave.
Jackson Heights

Rabbi Mendel Kaufman
84-75 Daniels St., Jamaica

Rabbi Bernard Rosensweig
82-17 Lefferts Blvd.
Kew Gardens

Rabbi B. Schiller
43 Frances Place, Monsey

Rabbi Moshe D. Tendler
2 Cloverdale Lane, Monsey

Rabbi Berel Wein
12 Hilltop Pl., Monsey

Rabbi S. Werner
6 Phyllis Ter., Monsey

Rabbi Joseph Chait
27 Sherman Ave., Mt. Vernon

Rabbi Solomon Freilich
Cong. Brothers of Israel
10 S. 8th Ave., Mt. Vernon

Rabbi Stanley Wexler
1228 North Ave., New Rochelle

Rabbi P. M. Weinberger
Cong. Anshe Sholom
50 North Ave., New Rochelle

Rabbi J. David Bleich
Cong. Bnai Yehuda
352 East 78 St., New York

Rabbi Label Dulitz
320 Wadsworth Ave., New York

Rabbi Emanuel Gettinger
210 West 91st St., New York

Rabbi Bernard Goldenberg
Torah Umesorah
229 Park Ave. South, N.Y.C.

Rabbi Leo Jung
131 West 86th St., New York

Rabbi Simon Langer
Cong. Orach Chaim
1459 Lexington Ave., N.Y.C.

Rabbi Haskel Lookstein
Cong. Kehilath Jeshurun
125 East 85th St., New York

Rabbi Yaakov Perlow
353 Ft. Washington Ave.
New York

Rabbi Eliezer Shapiro
39 Broadway, Suite 3202
New York

Rabbi Herman Shulman
120 Bennett Ave., New York

Rabbi Sherman D. Siff
229 East Broadway, New York

Rabbi Israel Wohlgelernter
3 West 16th St., New York

Rabbi Morris S. Gorelik
2428 Hamilton Road
No. Bellmore

Rabbi M. Davidowitz
Rabbi D. Harris
Talmudical Institute
759 Park Ave., Rochester

Rabbi S. Kalimnick
Cong. Beth Shalom
Monroe Ave., Rochester

Rabbi Yaakov Marcus
835 Forest Hill Road
Staten Island

Rabbi B. Emmer
201 Seeley Rd., Syracuse

Rabbi E. Glucksman
Ft. Wash. Ave., Wash. Hghts.
N.Y.C.

Rabbi S. Schwab
K'hal Adath Yeshurun
Washington Heights, N.Y.C.

Rabbi Sholom Gold
630 Hempstead Ave.
West Hempstead

Rabbi Nachum Laskin
Woodbourne

Rabbi Irving H. Goodman
Cong. Ohave Sholem
Woodridge

OHIO

Rabbi David Indich
Cincinnati

Rabbi Z. Sharfstein
1542 Beaverton, Cincinnati

Rabbi L. Alevsky
2004 S. Green Rd.
Cleveland

Dr. N. J. Klatzko
3536 Blanche, Cleveland

Rabbi Dr. M. Einstadter
3395 Blanche, Cleveland

Rabbi Yosie Abrams
3627 Harvey Road
Cleveland Heights

Rabbi C. Capland
57 E. 14th Ave., Columbus

Rabbi Marvin Possak
Cong. Ahavas Shalom, Columbus

Rabbi Avi Schwartz
Columbus

Rabbi David Stavsky
Cong. Beth Jacob
1223 College Ave., Columbus

Rabbi Edward H. Garsek
Cong. Etz Chaim
3853 Woodley Rd., Toledo

OREGON
Rabbi D. Rotenberg
2350 S.W. Vermont, Portland

PENNSYLVANIA
Rabbi David L. Silver
Kesher Israel Cong.
2500 North Third St.
Harrisburg

Rabbi Levin
Lower Merion Syn., Lower Merion

Rabbi Shlomo Caplan
Cong. Beth Hamedrosh
7505 Brookhaven Rd., Phila.

Rabbi Elya Svei
Rabbi Shmuel Kamenitsky
Yeshivah Philadelphia
6063 Drexel Rd., Phila.

Rabbi Irvin I. Chinn
Gemilas Chesed
1400 Summit St., McKeesport

Rabbi A. Shem Tov
7622 Castor Ave., Phila.

Rabbi Bernard A. Poupko
Shaare Torah Cong.
2319 Murray Ave., Pitt.

Rabbi K. Weiss
5614 Forbes Ave., Pitt.

Rabbi S. Katzen
5835 Nicholson St., Pitt.

Rabbi Michael B. Fine
441 Monroe Ave., Scranton

Rabbi Silverstein
652 Adams Ave., Scranton

RHODE ISLAND

Rabbi Avishai David
13 Taft St., Providence

Rabbi Sanford Pepper
262 Blackstone Blvd., Providence

TENNESSEE

Rabbi Meir Belsky
5225 Meadowcrest Cove
Memphis

Rabbi Zalman I. Posner
3600 West End Ave., Nashville

TEXAS

Rabbi Y. Loschak
2101 Nueces, Austin

Rabbi Alperowitz
5930 Harvest Hill, Dallas

Rabbi S. Lazaroff
109-50 Fondern, Houston

Rabbi Aryeh Scheinberg
115 E. Laurel
San Antonio

VERMONT

Rabbi S. Hecht
354 North St., Burlington

VIRGINIA

Rabbi Shaya Sakett
Norfolk

Rabbi Jacob Kranz
5311 W. Franklin St., Richmond

Rabbi D. Nelkin
5207 Monument Ave., Richmond

Rabbi K. Rosenbaum
4705 Augusta, Richmond

Rabbi S. Capland
901 F N Hamilton, Richmond

WASHINGTON

Rabbi S. Levitin
5215 S. Holly St., Seattle

Rabbi Moses Londinski
Bikur Cholim Machzikay Hadath
5140 South Morgan St., Seattle

Rabbi Solomon Maimon
52nd St. & South Morgan
Seattle

WISCONSIN

Rabbi Y. Hecht
613 Howard Pl., Madison

Rabbi David S. Shapiro
Cong. Anshe Sfard
3447 N. 51st Blvd., Milwaukee

Rabbi Yehudah Silver
N. 51st Blvd., Milwaukee

Rabbi I. Smotkin
2943 N. Summit, Milwaukee

Rabbi Tuvia Turem
5401 N. 54th St., Milwaukee

Rabbi Michael Twerski
3251 N. 51st Blvd.
Milwaukee

ARGENTINA

Rabbi Berl Baumgarten
Sarmiento 2318 1* 3
Buenos Aires

AUSTRALIA

Rabbi B. Cohen
Yeshivah Gedolah
67 Alexandra Rd.
E. St. Kilda, Melbourne

Rabbi Y. Groner
92 Hotham St.
E. St. Kilda, Melbourne

Rabbi P. Feldman
67A Penkiuil St.
Bondi, Sydney

BELGIUM

Rabbi S. Slabatitcky
44 Mercator St., Antwerp

Rabbi A. Chaikin
1A Ave. Rein Marie
Henriette, Brussels

BRAZIL

Rabbi R. Blumenfeld
Santa Clara 239-301
Rio de Janeiro

Rabbi Shabsi Alpern
60 Rua Chabad, San Paulo

CANADA

Rabbi Jay Braverman
4894 St. Kevin Ave.
Cote St. Luc, P.Q.

Rabbi B. Mockin
4387 Plamondon, Montreal

Rabbi M. Weinberg
Rabbi M. Levin
Rabbi R. Goldman
Yeshivah Gedolah
6155 Deacon Rd., Montreal

Rabbi M. Werner
6061 Wilderton, Montreal

Rabbi Mordechai Glick
2855 Victore Dore St., Montreal

Rabbi Moses J. Burak
Beth Jacob Cong.
147 Overbrook Place
Downsview, Ontario

Rabbi E. Lipsker
145 York Downs Drive
Downsview, Ontario

Rabbi J. I. Schochet
55 Charleswood Dr.
Downsview, Ontario

Rabbi D. Schochet
10 Romney Rd.
Downsview, Ontario

Dr. Y. Block
1059 Williams St.
London, Ontario

Rabbi M. Berger
690 Melbourne St., Ottawa

Rabbi Reuven P. Bulka
Cong. Machzikei Hadas
2310 Virginia Dr., Ottawa

Rabbi Alon
Ledbury Ave., Toronto

Rabbi Gedalia Felder
Shomrai Shabboth Synagogue
583 Glengrove Ave. W.
Toronto

Rabbi Henry Hoschander
Cong. Shaarei Shomayim
470 Glencairn Ave., Toronto

Rabbi S. N. Mandel
236 Carmichael Ave., Toronto

Rabbi Shlomo Miller
Stormont Ave., Toronto

Rabbi Irwin E. Witty
22 Glen Park Ave., Toronto

Rabbi Turin
Yeshivat Ner Yisroel
625 Finch Ave. W., Willowdale

Rabbi Chaim Nussbaum
6010 Bathurst St., Willowdale

Rabbi I. Wineberg
497 W. 39th
Vancouver, British Columbia

Rabbi A. Altien
532 Inkster Blvd.
Winnipeg, Manitoba

ENGLAND
Rabbi Shmuel Arkush
135 Pershore Rd., Birmingham

Rabbi Roni Mansoor
Edgware, Middlesex

Rabbi J. Grunfeld
Gateshead

Rabbi M. Salomon
16 Mindermere St., Gateshead

Rabbi Y. Angyalfi
594 Stonegate, Leeds

Rabbi D. Kass
Leeds

Rabbi B. Rapaport
Rabbi N. Roberg
Liverpool

Dayan A. D. Dunner
49 Craven Walk
London N16

Rabbi Dr. Joseph Freilich
7 Highcroft Gardens
London NW11

Rabbi Immanuel Jakobovits
Office of the Chief Rabbi
Tavistock Sq., London

Rabbi Shmuel Lew
Lubavitch Foundation
109-115 Stamford Hill
London N16

Rabbi N. L. Rabinovitch
40 The Downage
London NW4

Rabbi Roberg
Green Lane
London NW4

Rabbi Jonathan Sacks
31 Dunstan Rd.
London NW11

Rabbi N. Sudak
109-115 Stamford Hill
London N16

Rabbi Y. Balkind
Leicester Rd.
Salford, Manchester

Rabbi G. Brodie
43 Stanley Rd.
Salford, Manchester

Rabbi C. Farro
62 Singleton Rd.
Salford, Manchester

Rabbi M. Kupetz
4 Hanover Gardens
Salford, Manchester

FRANCE

Rabbi Israël
10, Place
Guynemer-Sarcelles

Rabbi Yaakov Toledano
17, Avenue Maurice
Le Raincy-Villemomble

Rabbi S. Gurewitz
3 Impasse Cazenoye
Lyon 69006

Rabbi Y. Y. Labkovsky
6 Parc Des Chuttes
Marseilles

Rabbi Y. Y. Pinson
24 bis Rue Berlioz
Nice 06100

Rabbi Shmuel Azimov
8 Rue Lamartine, Paris

Rabbi Frankforter
10, Rue Cadet, Paris

Rabbi Rottenberg
10, Rue Pavée, Paris

Rabbi Westheim
24, Rue des Martyrs, Paris

Rabbi Guershon Cahen
5, Rue Straus-Durkheim
Strasbourg

Rabbi Ita'h
44, Boulevard Clémenceau
Strasbourg

Rabbi Y. Y. Matusof
45 Bd. Lazare Carnot
Toulouse

HOLLAND

Rabbi B. Jacobs
101 Operaweg
Amemersfoort

Rabbi Y. Homnick
65 Beethoven St.
Amsterdam

Rabbi Chaim Hyams
Grevetingen St. 20
Amsterdam

ITALY

Rabbi Garelick
Via G. Ubert, 41, Milan

Rabbi I. Hazan
Via Lorenzo il Magnifico 23
Rome

MEXICO

Rabbi A. Bartfeld
Kehila Ashkenasi
Acapulco 70, Mexico City

Rabino Chaim Sued
Moliere 311 P.B.
Mexico 5 D.F.

MOROCCO

Rabbi Y. L. Raskin
10 Washington Ave.
Casablanca

SCOTLAND

Rabbi Chaim Jacobs
2 Elliot Ave.
Giffnock, Glasgow

SOUTH AFRICA

Rabbi M. Popack
31 Arthur's Rd.
Sea Point, Cape Town

Rabbi N. M. Bernhard
Oxford Syn.-Centre
20 North Avenue
Riviera, Johannesburg

Mr. Manny Cahn
Fortesque Road
Yeoville, Johannesburg

Rabbi S. Eisenblatt
24 Frances St.
Johannesburg

Rabbi B. Grosnass
"Ohr Yisrael"
Rabbi M. Fachler
Kollel "Yad Shaul"
48 Urania St.
Observatory, Johannesburg

Rabbi David Lapin
61 Garden Rd.
Orchards, Johannesburg

Rabbi Lipsker
33 Harley
Yeoville, Johannesburg

SWITZERLAND

Rabbi D. Levy
Israelitische Religions-gesellschaft
37 Freigutstrasse
Zurich

Rabbi M. Piron
Israelitische Cultus-gemeinde
Löwenstrass, Zurich

Rabbi H. Zahler
Mutschellenstrasse 55
Zurich, 8038

VENEZUELA

Rabbi Menashe Perman
Av. Los Proceres
Edif. Royal Palace Apt. 3
Caracas

WEST GERMANY

Rabbi M. Kaminker
Bogenstr. 27, Hamburg